To my friend & fellow [...] clergyman, Dr. Dennis Dickerson, thanks — & may God continue His blessings upon your labors
Randolph Meade Walker

P9-CDO-067

THE METAMORPHOSIS OF SUTTON E. GRIGGS:
THE TRANSITION FROM BLACK RADICAL TO CONSERVATIVE, 1913-1933

RANDOLPH MEADE WALKER

WALKER PUBLISHING

Memphis, 1991

© 1990

Randolph Meade Walker

i

Dedication

It is with gratitude that I dedicate this work to the memory of my mother and father, the late Elsie and Levi Walker, whose early support and tutelage made this possible.

TABLE OF CONTENTS

LIST OF TABLES

LIST OF FIGURES

ACKNOWLEDGMENTS

This work was made possible by aids given the author by numerous contributors. The earliest encouragement that was given the author to pursue Sutton E. Griggs' career as an extended topic of study came from Dr. Charles W. Crawford, my major professor at Memphis State University. His constant nurturing and guiding made the effort attainable.

Likewise the author wishes to express his gratitude to the other members of his dissertation committee: Dr. C. Edward Skeen, Dr. Major L. Wilson, Dr. Walter R. Brown, and Dr. Abraham Kriegel, who was kind enough to take the place of the late Dr. Marcus W. Orr. Their critical reading and helpful comments have enhanced the work's worth.

The author is appreciative of assistance he received from the library staffs at the John W. Brister Library, the Memphis/Shelby County Public Library and Information Center, and the Hollis F. Price Library. All of these libraries always provided assistance to even the most speculative requests.

Likewise there were a number of institutions beyond Memphis that provided valuable material in the author's research. Therefore the support given by the following is acknowledged: The Historical Commission of the Southern Baptist Convention, the Moorland-Spingarn Research Center at Howard University, the libraries at Texas Southern University, Duke University, Union Theological Seminary (New York), and California State University at Northridge.

The author is grateful to Ms. Carolyn Jeffries and Ms. Janice Cook. The former typed the earlier drafts, while the latter did the final.

Last, but not least, the author is grateful for an understanding family. His wife, Deloris, and children, Jennifer and John were deprived of his company while this work was in the making. Without their cooperation this labor would have never reached fruition.

FOREWORD

Sutton E. Griggs was one of the most published black authors in the early years of the twentieth century. Unfortunately he has been given only scant attention. The majority of the studies on his views have only considered his early fictional writings. Consequently, only a partial view of Griggs' contributions have been considered by most scholars.

Due to this dearth of information on the total contributions of Griggs, this study attempts to trace the philosophical changes that took place in the writer. Griggs, a man of many talents, was also a clergyman and the founding spirit of the American Baptist Theological Seminary in Nashville, Tennessee. After relocating to Memphis in 1913, he abandoned his earlier apologetic stance against the anti-black propaganda that swept the country following Reconstruction. After 1913 his philosophy was dominated by his accommodationist espousal of "social efficiency."

The main thrust of this study is to determine why this change took place. A thorough examination of Griggs' writings and a consideration of his era are analyzed in reaching a conclusion. In regards to the latter factor, the investigation demonstrates how even an intellectual black activist became a victim of Eurocentric teachings about world civilization. This indoctrination helped to influence his view of his own people and the strategy he advocated for the uplift of the newly emancipated Americans of African descent.

As to style, the author feels obligated to orientate the reader to certain words employed throughout the book. The terms "black", "Negro," and "African American" are used interchangeably. The rationale for this is an effort is made to capture some of the historical flavor of citations. Also, at the same time the work does attempt to be sensitive to contemporary preference through the employment of the more recent term "African American." Finally, the author confesses that the variety is a matter of taste. Variation in terminology is preferred by the author, rather than the monotonous overemployment of the same word throughout the work.

Where specialized language is used, explanatory footnotes have been employed. Hopefully, their inclusion will serve as a boon to those who may find some terms vague or confusing.

It is this same aspiration for clarity that has led to the inclusion of tables and illustrations. It is the author's desire that the reader will find the pictures and tables worth a thousand words. Likewise an appendix with additional photographs is included to aid the reader in fully understanding the times of Sutton E. Griggs.

Finally, it is hoped the reader will find reading about Sutton E. Griggs as fascinating as the author found him to be as a research and writing topic. May the reader find some of his views worth retaining as the author did.

Randolph Meade Walker
LeMoyne-Owen College

INTRODUCTION

Sutton E. Griggs was a man who contributed so much about which posterity knows so little. This ignorance of the man is most evident in the change that Griggs underwent after he became domiciled in Memphis, Tennessee, in 1913. Prior to that event Griggs was one of America's most outspoken African American apologists. He especially was critical of the South's treatment of the black American.

Rare for his day, Griggs was one of the few African Americans who wrote numerous books on the subject of race relations. In his early years his mission was to defend black people from the assaults that were launched by a deluge of anti-black propagandists at the end of the nineteenth and the beginning of the twentieth centuries.

Due to his literary rebellion at a time when such positions were grounds for southern lynchings, sketchy studies have portrayed him as a radical. These studies have failed to see him as a maturing thinker. Most of these studies have only considered his early writings.

In 1975 David Tucker in a chapter in his book *Black Pastors and Leaders* did explore Griggs' life long enough to discover the minister's metamorphosis. However, failing to look at Griggs' writings in depth, Tucker prematurely concludes that Griggs was motivated by less than honorable intentions for his change in approaching the race issue. Tucker believes that Griggs' integrity was bought by Memphis whites. In his view it is the power of "filthy lucre" that transforms the radical Griggs into an accommodationist.

After having read several of Sutton Griggs' early books, such as *Wisdom's Call, Unfettered, The One Great Question, Imperio in Imperio,* and *The Hindered Hand,* it became apparent to the author that something more than money had to inspire the change in Griggs. A perusal of the post 1913 publications confirmed the early suspicions that the later Griggs was as profound a thinker as he was as a young man. Consequently, it only seemed logical that a deeper investigation would reveal that no study had seriously followed the minister's philosophy from its genesis through its conclusion.

Furthermore, it seemed a terrible oversight in history that no thorough study had been done on the full contributions of one who had written so much on the race issue. Indeed, it is long past due that posterity should closely and completely trace the career and thoughts of Sutton E. Griggs. This is the object of this study. Along the sojourn, it is anticipated that clues to the cause of the southern, black, Baptist minister's metamorphosis will be uncovered.

CHAPTER I

Anti-Black Propaganda

When Confederate General Robert E. Lee surrendered to Union General Ulysses S. Grant at Appomattox, Virginia, in 1865, the Civil War formally came to an end. Yet, this single act by no means terminated hostility between the North and South. The former Confederacy refused to lay aside its differences with the Union. During the last quarter of the nineteenth and the beginning of the twentieth centuries, Confederate sympathizers employed the pen rather than the musket to fire pro-southern volleys.

Caught in the midst of this propaganda war was the black American. He was made a favorite scapegoat for all the evils the country had known during its internal fighting. These writers blamed the Negro for every misfortune that the South had suffered in the past or could anticipate suffering in the future.

This literature was produced at a time when the nation needed healing. However, these publications served as irritants to old wounds. Racist sentiments were inspired in many quarters as a result of these messages. Lynching and black disfranchisement took place simultaneously with this corpus of racist writings.

The anti-black propagandists wrote in both a fictional and nonfictional format.[1] Two of the most infamous, prolific writers from the black man's perspective were the Reverend Thomas Dixon, Jr. and Thomas Nelson Page. The former's favorite medium was the novel, while the latter wrote social, educational, and political treatises. Dixon clearly was the blunter of the two, while Page used a more persuasive, intellectual approach. Despite the different approaches to the Negro question, their conclusion was identical — the black man was inferior.

A favorite theme of this anti-black literature was the beneficence of southern slavery. For example, the termination of slavery was often cited as an end to intimacy between the races.[2] Since post-bellum blacks were no longer compelled to have close contact with whites, this lack of association was cited by the writers as a reason for the absence of progress by the former.[3] Thus, they argued slavery was not so bad after all. In fact, according to these slavery apologists, it actually worked to the good of Africans brought to America.

> Slavery, whatever its demerits, was not in its time the unmitigated evil it is fancied to have been. Its time has passed. No power could compel the South to have it back. But to the Negro it was salvation. It found him a savage and a cannibal and in two hundred years gave seven millions of his race a civilization, the only civilization it has had since the dawn of history.[4]

1

This propaganda attempted to portray slavery not as exploitative, but indeed redemptive. Furthermore, such redemption was predicated upon a very negative view of African history. These arguments thus rested squarely upon the assumption that Negro inferiority was a self-evident fact. One of the anti-black writers said, "It may be stated, however, that, notwithstanding exceptional instances, the case of the South rests frankly on the present demonstrable inferiority of the Negro race to the White race."[5] Indeed, in the eyes of such penmen the Negro was done a great disservice by those who would tutor him in the realm of universal equality.[6]

Employing a fictional character, one anti-black novel cited the generally favorite proof of African inferiority.

> Education, sir, is the development of that which is. Since the dawn of history the Negro has owned the Continent of Africa—rich beyond the dream of poet's fancy, crunching acres of diamonds beneath his bare black feet. Yet he never picked one up from the dust until a white man showed to him its glittering light. His land swarmed with powerful and docile animals, yet he never dreamed a harness, cart, or sled. A hunter by necessity, he never made an axe, spear, or arrowhead worth preserving beyond the moment of its use. He lived as an ox, content to graze for an hour. In a land of stone and timber he never sawed a foot of lumber, carved a block, or built a house save of broken sticks and mud. With league on league of ocean strand and miles of inland seas, for four thousand years he watched their surface ripple under the wind, heard the thunder of the surf on his beach, the howl of the storm over his head, gazed on the dim blue horizon calling him to worlds that lie beyond, and yet he never dreamed a sail! He lived as his fathers lived—stole his food, worked his wife, sold his children, ate his brother, content to drink, sing, dance, and sport as the ape.[7]

Such a fictionalized, polemic narration helped to feed ideas of white supremacy. The supremacy was built around the notion that the black American's African heritage was something worthless and degrading. Africa was depicted as a wild, uncivilized, savage land.

These anti-black writers went beyond polemics in their teachings on Negro inferiority. They portrayed the physical features of the black man as subhuman. In an early twentieth century novel, the following description was given of an African American soldier:

> He had the short, heavy-set neck of the lower order of animals. His skin was coal black, his lips so thick they curled both ways up and down with crooked blood marks across them. His nose was flat, and its enormous nostrils seemed in perpetual dilation. The sinister bead eyes, with brown splotches in their whites, were set wide apart and gleamed apelike under his scant brows. His enormous cheekbones and jaws seemed to protrude beyond the ears and almost hide them.[8]

Needless to say, such descriptions gave the impression that blacks were not human. This was a blatant attack upon the Negro's humanity. Such writings helped to foster the idea that blacks were an alien species from whites. Indeed, such literature even made appeals to the suggested animal traits of blacks.

This was the overt racist writing that was easily identified for its hostility toward those of African descent. However, the anti-black literature of the period also assumed more subtle forms as well. In a treatise on the racial question, one southerner wrote:

> It is not argued that because a Negro is a Negro he is incapable of any intel-lectual development. On the contrary, observation has led me to think that under certain conditions of intellectual environment, of careful training, and of sympathetic encouragement from the stronger races he may individually attain a fair, and in uncommon instances a considerable degree of mental development. To deny this is to deny the highest attribute of the intellectual essence, and is to shut the door of hope upon a race of God's human crea-tures to whom I give my sympathy and my good-will.[9]

This type of writing attempted to disguise its message of racism. Despite its attempt, the message clearly is an appeal to the concept of white man's burden. The writer's "sympathy" and "good-will" were predicated upon a paternalistic attitude. Furthermore, those black Americans who did succeed intellectually were credited by the writer for doing so because of the contacts that whites had with them. In essence, the Negro could do nothing of note on his own. He was a ward of the European American.

This idea of Negro inequality disposed the southerner to interpret Re-construction as a preposterous affair. Most white southerners saw Re-construction as a time of "Negro Rule."[10] Whether this was actually the case or not was immaterial to the Confederate apologists who wrote of the audacity of the federal government in placing blacks over whites during Reconstruction. In a novel, the following reference to radical Re-construction was made:

> It seemed a joke sometimes as he thought of it, a huge, preposterous joke, this actual attempt to reverse the order of nature, turn society upside down, and make a thick-lipped, flat-nosed negro but yesterday taken from the jungle, the ruler of the proudest and strongest race of men evolved in two thousand years of history.[11]

The writer took for granted that blacks were inferior to whites. This biased interpretation of Reconstruction made the period appear topsy-turvy to him. In his mind, it was a period of an illogical arrangement, which made radical Reconstruction a ludicrous affair to these anti-black writers.

In addition to the period appearing ridiculous, as far as the pro-south-erners were concerned, so did those whites who befriended blacks. Both carpetbaggers and scalawags were dismissed as impossible schemers. In his notorious novel, *The Clansman: An Historical Romance of the Ku Klux Klan,* Thomas Dixon, Jr. used the "Old Commoner" as an obvious representative of Thaddeus Stevens. The "Old Commoner" is portrayed as a betrayer of the white race and a dupe of his mulatto housekeeper.

The southern apologist saw Reconstruction as a conspiracy between Negroes and unscrupulous whites. These writers regarded the whites who befriended blacks as self-serving soldiers of fortune. On the other hand, blacks were seen as gullible and an easy prey of such whites.

In another of his novels, *The Leopard's Spots: A Romance of the White Man's Burden—1865-1900,* Thomas Dixon, Jr. cast Simon Legree (of

Harriet Beecher Stowe's *Uncle Tom's Cabin*) as a scalawag. Legree, with Tim Shelby, a Negro demagogue, formed an alliance to exploit the South. By casting the infamous slave owner, in this role, Dixon attempted to show the infantile vulnerability of the black American. According to such representation, the childlike, simple Negro was used during Reconstruction by the most reprehensible slaver of all.

Such characterizations underlay three of Dixon's goals. First, he attempted to show that the Negro was not perceptive and therefore was easily manipulated. Second, he tried to demonstrate that the southern scalawag was indeed a selfish, unprincipled schemer, and an aberration from the southern norm. Third, but not least important, Dixon portrayed the white South as a victim of Reconstruction. Together, ignorant Negroes and unprincipled whites took advantage of the post-bellum South.

As a result, anti-black propagandists argued that the birth of the Ku Klux Klan was a necessary defensive move by the white South. Dixon described the genesis of this controversial organization as follows:

> The simple truth is, it [the Klan] was a spontaneous and resistless racial uprising of clansmen of highland origin living along the appalachian mountains and foothills of the South, and it appeared almost simultaneously in every Southern state produced by the same terrible conditions.[12]

Of course, the "terrible conditions" to which Dixon makes reference were the perceived victimization of the white South. Consequently, such writers romanticized and made heroes out of southern vigilantes, who not only took the law into their own hands, but instituted a haven for white supremacy.

The withdrawal of federal troops from the South officially signaled the end of Reconstruction. This action was cheered by Dixon. His appreciation for the withdrawal was given in the following manner:

> Negro refugees and their associates once more filled the ear of the national government with clamor for the return of the army to the South to uphold Negro power, but for the first time since 1867, it fell on deaf ears. The Anglo-Saxon race had been reunited. The Negro was no longer the ward of the Republic. Henceforth, he must stand or fall on his own worth and pass under the law of the survival of the fittest.[13]

The last phrase is an interesting allusion to Social Darwinism.

It was during this period that Charles Darwin's biological theories were transferred to the social arena.[14] The evolutionary notion of the survival of the fittest was used as a justification for racism and imperialism.

The strange irony of this was that the Protestant fundamental Bible Belt welcomed Social Darwinism as a strategic tool to justify its racism. Yet, it was this same constitutency that later provided the court challenge to the teaching of the evolutionary theory.

To justify violence against blacks and the strict restriction placed upon them, the anti-black propagandists catered to Negrophobia. They constantly played upon southern fears of what the Negro would do as a free individual. A favorite warning was that the Negro would violate the white

4

woman. In 1904, Thomas Nelson Page echoed this scare tactic by writing, "Today, no white woman, or girl, or female child goes alone out of sight of the house except on necessity; and no man leaves his wife alone in his house, if he can help it."[15]

Such depictions portrayed the black man as an animalistic, sex-crazed psychopath, who innately craved white women. These writers claimed the black man was incapable of exercising morality and self-control when it came to the opposite sex. Page declared:

> In the first place, the Negro does not generally believe in the virtue of women. It is beyond his experience. He does not generally believe in the existence of actual assault. It is beyond his comprehension. In the next place, his passion, always his controlling force, is now, since the new teaching, for the white women.[16]

The new teaching to which Page made reference was that of equality. Page and others warned the white South that the doctrine of racial equality would be interpreted by black men as a license to an equal helping of the white woman.

As Page's treatises created southern hysteria over the black man's freedom, so did Dixon's novels. Repeatedly, in his writings the subplot of a beastly Negro attacking white women and girls was employed.

Such propaganda inflamed the white southerner's imagination. He became paranoid and suspicious of every black male. Such emotions fed an appetite for violence and bloodshed. Throughout the South (and some parts of the North) blacks were lynched with a calloused frequency.

From Table 1 it can be seen that it was not until 1886 that there were more Negroes lynched than whites. From that date forward it is evident that blacks were far more likely to be victims of vigilante attacks. Between 1886 and 1922, save only for the interruption of World War I in 1917, there were at least 50 black lynchings annually. These same years (1886-1922) composed the period in which the bulk of the anti-black propaganda was issued.

Despite the fact that Thomas Nelson Page found evidence that some lynching involved cases of mistaken identity,[17] he still wrote apologetically of the white South's employment of the brutal practice. He stated with absolute certainty that the way to reduce lynching was for blacks to become civilized to the point that they ceased to assault white females.[18] Contrary to the American legal system, such claims assumed the black man was "guilty until proven innocent."

Armed with such assumptions, the anti-black propagandists defended the South's use of violence. In their view, it was neither extravagant nor unreasonable. While Dixon defended such practices with an emotional appeal, Page employed a pseudo-rational approach. Whichever method was used, the resulting conclusion was the same—the black man was an undisciplined threat to white females that could only be controlled by force.

The propagandists supplemented this myth with another element of

5

Table 1
Series H 1168-1170. Persons Lynched, by Race: 1882 to 1970
(no lynchings occurred in 1952-1954, 1956, 1958, 1960, 1962, and 1965-1970)

Year	Total 1168	White 1169	Negro 1170	Year	Total 1168	White 1169	Negro 1170
1964[1]	3	2	1	1919	83	7	76
1963.	1	—	1	1918	64	4	60
1961.	1	—	1	1917	38	2	36
1959.	1	—	1	1916	54	4	50
1957.	1	1	—	1915	69	13	56
1955.	8	—	8	1914	55	4	51
1951.	1	—	1	1913	52	1	51
1950.	2	1	1	1912	63	2	61
1949.	3	—	3	1911	67	7	60
1948.	2	1	1	1910	76	9	67
1947.	1	—	1	1909	82	13	69
1946.	6	—	6	1908	97	8	89
1945.	1	—	1	1907	60	2	58
1944.	2	—	2	1906	65	3	62
1943.	3	—	3	1905	62	5	57
1942.	6	—	6	1904	83	7	76
1941.	4	—	4	1903	99	15	84
1940.	5	1	4	1902	92	7	85
1939.	3	1	2	1901	130	25	105
1938.	6	—	6	1900	115	9	106
1937.	8	—	8	1899	106	21	85
1936.	8	—	8	1898	120	19	101
1935.	20	2	18	1897	158	35	123
1934.	15	—	15	1896	123	45	78
1933.	28	4	24	1895	179	66	113
1932.	8	2	6	1894	192	58	184
1931.	13	1	12	1893	152	34	118
1930.	21	1	20	1892	230	69	161
1929.	10	3	7	1891	184	71	113
1928.	11	1	10	1890	96	11	86
1927.	16	—	16	1889	170	76	94
1926.	30	7	23	1888	137	68	69
1925.	17	—	17	1887	120	50	70
1924.	16	—	16	1886	138	64	74
1923.	33	4	29	1885	184	110	74
1922.	57	6	51	1884	211	160	51
1921.	64	5	59	1883	130	77	58
1920.	61	8	53	1882	113	64	49

—Represents zero. 1 No lynchings, 1965-1970

U.S. Department of Commerce, Bureau of the Census. Historical Statistics of the United States; Colonial Times to 1970. Washington: Government Printing Office, 1975.

Negrophobia. They espoused the belief that miscegenation would result in a hybrid race that would be unacceptable by the standards of decency and excellence. Repeatedly in *The Leopard's Spots,* Dixon warned that the future of the country was at stake. The mixing of the races in his view would produce certain disaster. Therefore, he thundered, "the country will either be Anglo-Saxon or Mulatto."[19] One drop of Negro blood means a Negro.

Again, this argument can be clearly seen as having a Darwinian connection. Survival of the fittest was the propagandists' objective. In their view the most "fit" were the white race. Therefore, to keep it fit they wanted it "pure", free of any other race's blood, especially that of the Negro.

Indeed, it was ironic that in the same breath they defended slavery, which had fostered the greatest miscegenation of all time. It was because of the vulnerability of the black female during slavery that a large mulatto population had been born. The propagandists said nothing against the assaults that white men perpetrated upon these helpless black women.

Negrophobia was used in predicting the future. Page forecast that the American black population would be sixty to eighty million by the end of the twentieth century. In desperation he asked, "What shall be done with this colored population of sixty to eighty millions of souls?"[20] Such a question clearly conveyed to the panic-stricken South that things would get worse as the black population grew.

Such inflammatory predictions helped perpetuate the determination to oppress the African American. If the dark skinned American was viewed as a growing menace, then whites could be expected to do all in their power to terminate this anticipated danger.

When it came to the attacks launched by the anti-black propagandists, nothing in the African American culture was sacred or exempt from criticism. In Dixon's *The Leopard's Spots,* Nelse, a faithful former slave, speaks disdainfully about the black congregations which were organized after the Civil War:

> So dey's got ole Uncle Josh Miller to preach fur'em. He'low he got er call, en he stan'up dar en holler fur'em bout er hour ev'ry Sunday mawnin'en night. En sech whoopin; en yellin, 'en bawlin'! Yer can hear'em er mile. Dey tries ter git me ter go. I tell'em, Marse John Durham's preachin's good ernuf fur me, gall'ry er no gall'ry. I tell'em dat I spec er gall'ry nigher heaven den de lower flow enyhow-en fuddermo; dat when I goes ter church, I wants ter hear sumfin-mo'dan er ole fool nigger er bawlin: I can holler myself.[21]

Needless to say, this representation helped to undermine the credibility of the black church and its clergy[22] in the eyes of the white South. The stereotype of a buffoon in the pulpit of the black church was nurtured by such a characterization.

In addition to the books written by Page and Dixon, there were other anti-black publications. The mere title of Charles Carroll's *The Negro: A Beast* readily displayed the author's opinion of the black man. Such assumed inferiority of Negroes was frequently repeated by various writers of the time. Edward Eggleston bluntly said that the Negro's intellect

> ...when compared with the higher caucasian, is meagre indeed, and that something more than the mere ability to imitate and copy, in a parrot fash-

Figure 1. Paul Laurence Dunbar

> ion, some infinitesimal portion of our accumulated knowledge is requisite
> for the uplift of this alien and barbarous not to say savage, race of mankind.[23]

It is most evident that Eggleston saw no connection whatsoever between blacks and whites. In his view, blacks were simply a foreign entity incapable of original thought.

Furthermore, Philip Bruce contended that progress of any type was an impossibility for the African American. Unlike some of his contemporaries, Bruce did not even believe that association with whites helped bring a higher form of civilization to blacks. His rigid view of Negro inferiority is seen in the following statement:

> Their original spirit as a race has not been radically modified by transplantation to the American continent, the vigor and tenacity of their fundamental qualities having only grown more clearly perceptible with the progress of time, these fundamental qualities appearing to be incapable of alteration, however favorable circumstances may be to it.[24]

Here the anti-black propagandist inflicts a double wound upon the African American. In addition to his pronouncement that blacks are hopelessly lost in a state of mediocrity, he implies that American slavery was a favorable circumstance in which Negroes were placed. Thus, in Bruce's view there was no difference between blacks. Whether one was a common laborer, preacher, or teacher, they were all the same from his perspective. Bruce contended that training had no effect upon the Negro, because he was forever innately inferior.[25]

There was so much anti-black propaganda that the writers could not even agree among themselves in their arguments to prove Negro inferiority. For example, Frederick L. Hoffman vigorously protested any form of race mixing. He considered a mixed child as inferior to either its white father or black mother.[26] On the other hand, Eggleston declared that those Negroes who attained distinction were not really Negroes. He declared that they were of mixed ancestry and it was the European parentage that enabled the mulatoo to excel. Among these mixed distinguished persons he listed Alexandre Dumas, Frederick Douglass, W. E. B. DuBois, William H. Lewis (assistant Attorney—General of the United States), and Booker T. Washington. He even included the poet "Paul Lawrence (sic.) Dunbar", though Eggleston admits that "it does not appear that any of his ancestors were white."[27] Yet, to justify the inclusion, the anti-black propagandist says, "but coming from a race of slaves it is quite impossible to prove that such was or was not the case."[28]

From Figure 1 we can see that the physical features of the poet bear no resemblance whatsoever to those of Europeans.[29] Physical evidence notwithstanding, the anti-black propagandist attempted to weave him into a list of those who had infusions of European blood, which contributed to their talents. Such ancestral thievery was done in order to substantiate Eggleston's thesis that declared, "We are not sure there has ever lived a pure Negro exceptionally distinguished for his intellectual powers."[30]

As degrading as the books were, they were not the only organ of publicity that presented a sub-human portrait of the African American. Newspapers in their routine reporting projected a bigoted image of the black man. An example of this can be seen especially in stories where black men were accused of molesting white women or children. In Memphis *The Commercial Appeal* gave the following account of an incident that took place in Mayfield, Kentucky on January 12, 1898:

> Bob Blanks, a noted negro character, outraged the 11-year-old daughter of Mrs. Gertie Bailey at 7 o'clock tonight, in the western part of the city. Mrs. Bailey sent her two children to a neighbor's house, and while on their way to the place Blanks seized the eldest one and dragged her into a cellar, where he committed the fiendish act. The accompanying sister gave the alarm, and an officer arrived and fired at the negro as he fled. A large mob is in hot pursuit, and a neck-tie social will surely occur if the brute is captured.[31]

The article sets forth a presumption of guilt before any kind of trial takes place. In fact, the last sentence suggests that a lynching was the anticipated norm for such accusations. In addition, the white community's passion for revenge was increased by the newspaper's labelling of the suspect as a brute. This legitimated the mob's violence by convincing them they were not going to kill a man, but a beast.

Magazines likewise contained degrading reporting on the African American. In the September, 1899 issue of *Nineteenth Century,* Elizabeth Banks defended southern Jim Crow practices because she believed the Negro to be a brute.[32] Therefore, she wrote that the Negro must be excluded from general public accomodations because he lacked manners and the proper hygiene to be accorded a place of acceptance in America.

Likewise, the so-called scholarly journals of the day echoed the same theme of Negro inferiority. The historian, Ulrich B. Phillips wrote in the *Sewanee Review* issue of July, 1904:

> The conditions of our problem are as follows: (1) A century or two ago the negroes were savages in the wilds of Africa, (2) Those who were brought to America, and their descendants, have acquired a certain amount of civilization, and are now in some degree fitted for life in modern civilized society, (3) This progress of the negroes has been in very large measure the result of their association with civilized white people, (4) An immense mass of the negroes is sure to remain for an indefinite period in the midst of a civilized white nation. The problem is, How can we best provide for their peaceful residence and their further progress in this nation of white men? and how can we best guard against their lapsing back into barbarism? As a possible solution for a large part of the problem, I suggest the plantation system.[33]

Phillips' ideas were paternalistic and undergirded with a subscription to a belief in white man's burden. Furthermore, he predicated his favorable view of slavery as a civilizing force upon the notion that Africans had no history worthy of mention. His concept of the continent was the same negative picture that Page and Dixon reflected in their writings. Consequently, whether one consulted the historian or the novelist, he found the venom of anti-black propaganda.

Perhaps most damaging of all was D. W. Griffith's movie version of Dixon's novel, *The Clansman.* It was released in 1916 under its widely known title *The Birth of a Nation.* The movie reached not only the reading public, but the semi-literate and the illiterate as well. Its message was so potent that practically everywhere it played, racial unrest was sure to follow.

Indeed, the poison of the anti-black propagandists reached far into the American psyche during the late nineteenth and early twentieth centuries. The propagandists took advantage of prejudice, fear, and ignorance to increase the nation's racial polarization. They had a wide audience even though there were contradictions[34] and factual errors in their message.

Yet, despite their appeal, they did not go unchallenged. The anti-black propagandists set the stage for the black response.

NOTES

[1]From a factual, scientific, historical approach we could in reality call both propagandists' messages fictional.

[2]It was not even considered by these writers that slavery's intimacy was not one based on equality. Indeed, the intimacy was based upon southern white paternalism.

[3]For an example of this position, see Thomas Nelson Page, *The Negro: The Southerner's Problem* (New York: Scribner, 1904).

[4]*Ibid.*, p. 285.

[5]*Ibid.*, p. 127.

[6]*Ibid.*

[7]Thomas Dixon, Jr., *The Clansman: An Historical Romance of the Ku Klux Klan* (New York: Grosset & Dunlap, 1905), p. 292.

[8]*Ibid.*, p. 216.

[9]Page, p. 250.

[10]This interpretation mainly derived from the passage of the Reconstruction Act of 1867, which included the "iron clad oath", which disfranchised many ex-Confederates. For a full treatment of this subject, see John Hope Franklin and Alfred A. Moss, Jr., *From Slavery to Freedom: History of Negro Americans* (6th ed.; New York: Alfred A. Knopf, 1980), pp. 216-223.

[11]Thomas Dixon, Jr., *The Leopard's Spots; A Romance of the White Man's Burden—1865-1900* (New York: Doubleday, Page & Co., 1902), p. 97.

[12]*Ibid.*, p. 150.

[13]*Ibid.*, p. 414.

[14]For a definitive treatment of this transition see Richard Hofstadter, *Social Darwinism in American Thought* (Revised ed.; Boston: Beacon Press, 1955).

[15]Page, p. 97.

[16]*Ibid.*, p. 112.

[17]*Ibid.*, p. 91.

[18]See the chapter on lynching in *Ibid.*

[19]Dixon, *The Leopard's Spots*, pp. 159, 198, 438.

[20]Page, p. 289.

[21]Dixon, *The Leopard's Spots*, p. 41.

[22]The concept that the black church is anti-intellectual is even prevalent among some black scholars. For example, see E. Franklin Frazier, *The Negro Church in America* (New York: Schocken Books, 1964), p. 86.

[23]Edward Eggleston, *The Ultimate Solution of the American Negro Problem* (Boston: The Gorham Press, 1913), p. 63.

[24]Philip A. Bruce, *The Plantation Negro as a Freeman* (New York: G. P. Putnam's Sons, 1889), p. 126.

[25]*Ibid.*, p. 127.

[26]Frederick L. Hoffman, *Race Traits and Tendencies of the American Negro* (New York: The MacMillan Company, 1896), p. 180.

[27]Eggleston, p. 252.

[28]*Ibid.*

[29]Modern scholars believe the poet was of pure black African ancestry.

[30]Eggleston, p. 251.

[31]*The Commercial Appeal*, January 13, 1898, p. 1.

[32]Elizabeth L. Banks, "The American Negro and His Place," *Nineteenth Century*, September, 1899, pp. 459-74.

[33]Ulrich B. Phillips, "The Plantation as a Civilizing Factor," Sewanee Review, XII (July, 1904), 258.

[34]An example of the contradictions is found in Dixon, *The Leopard's Spots.* He contended that education of any sort should not be wasted on the Negro. He argued it will not change the black man's basic nature anymore than "the Leopard can change his spots or the Ethiopian his color." Yet, he then stated the Negro must not be given agricultural or industrial training because this would make him master of the South.

CHAPTER II

The Black Response

It was certainly within reason to expect a black American response to the anti-black propagandists. Blacks were placed in a position where they had to refute the stinging indictments made against their race. A defense was not an option but a necessity. African Americans had to neutralize the racist literary attacks with their own literary works.

A written defense was needed first to eradicate the negative stereotypes that had been circulated against the humanity of the black man. If blacks were ever to be accepted as human beings, they had to set their case forth logically and methodically in print. Otherwise, it might be interpreted by the public as proof that the African American was incapable of meeting his opponent on the literary field of battle, thus, proving the black man's innate inferiority.

Aside from this need to persuade others, the black American had to write for his own sake as well. Black intellectuals had to write books (fiction and nonfiction), and newspaper and magazine articles that told their story in a respectable manner. The black American could not be expected to have a favorable impression of himself as long as all he read depicted his race as subhuman.

Consequently, the African American response was as much for the self-image of black people as it was to persuade others. If the black mind was only exposed to the distortions of Thomas Dixon, Thomas Nelson Page, and others, then the black man would conceive of himself as worthless, and innately corrupt.

If a positive self-image was to be cultivated, another interpretation of African history needed to be shown than the bigoted way Dixon and Page had portrayed the native land of the dark-hued American. African history must be recorded accurately and not left to the pens of self-serving bigots who wrote from a prejudiced viewpoint.

Indeed, after the publications of the anti-black propagandists, a black literary response had to come forth. The intellectual survival of a people was at stake. Without a written defense, others, and African Americans themselves would look upon anything black or African as evil and undesirable.[1]

There were many blacks who began to see the need for the black perspective to be incorporated in literature. For example, refusal by the American Baptist Publications Society to accept black writers' material led the all black National Baptist Convention to make plans to establish its own publishing house in Nashville, Tennessee, in 1896. This enterprise enabled Sunday School literature to be written, published, and distributed by Negroes to Negroes, demonstrating a strong desire for the African American view to be reflected in the literature read and studied by the black church.

Some black Baptist congregations however, continued to use the materials published by white organizations.[2] In the September 1897 session of the National Baptist Convention, U.S.A., a considerable amount of debate centered around "the use of American Baptist literature and cooperation with white Baptists in general."[3] This debate was mainly along state lines. The delegates from Virginia and North Carolina were favorably disposed to buying white Baptists' literature and working with them. In the case of the latter state, the American Baptist Home Mission Society (white) had done much to aid the beginnings of black Baptist efforts in the Tar Heel state. Thus, the delegates felt indebted to their white brethren and were not prepared to renounce their interracial cooperations. The debate gave birth to the Lott Carey Baptist Home and Foreign Mission Convention, which was organized in Shiloh Baptist Church, Washington, D.C. in 1897. The new convention consisted exclusively of east coast congregations, with North Carolina and Virginia at its core.

Despite the dissension, the fact that the National Baptist Convention, U.S.A. had previously created its own publishing arm demonstrated a growing awareness by blacks that they needed to publish their own views. This denominational enterprise was therefore part of a larger black aspiration.

African Americans of all denominations, as well as some with no denominational identity, began to oppose the anti-black propagandists with the aid of a blossoming of black American intellectuals who wrote from a black perspective. In doing so, they challenged the propaganda of the white supremacists.

The black American had reached a point where he made known his displeasure with racism. The voice of protest was so readily accepted that the Woman's Department of the National Baptist Convention in 1915 voiced displeasure over southern laws that prevented whites from teaching in black schools.[4]

William Edward Burghardt DuBois was indisputedly the foremost black intellectual of the era. In 1895 he attained the distinction of becoming the first Negro to earn a Ph.D. degree from Harvard University. He was not only a prolific producer of scholarly articles and books; he was also a history maker himself. DuBois was one of the founders of the National Association for the Advancement of Colored People in 1909. He also served as editor of that organization's official magazine, *Crisis.*

Early in the twentieth century, DuBois gained recognition as a black spokesman when he openly disagreed with the influential accommodationist policies of Booker T. Washington. In contrast to Washington,

DuBois publicly advocated complete racial equality, an anti-lynching posture, and a liberal arts education for the talented tenth of his race.

In addition to his bold stance and activities, DuBois refuted the anti-black propagandists by writing about history, sociology, education, and economics from a scholarly African American point of view. DuBois reinterpreted such events as Reconstruction and the African slave trade. DuBois' massive volume, *Black Reconstruction in America, 1860-1880* is a well written, superbly documented, revisionist study of the Negro's role in such a critical period in the country's history. In the last chapter, entitled "The Propaganda of History," DuBois did a role call of anti-black Reconstruction histories. He exposed those works that evolved from an anti-black thesis and built it up with emotional appeals, rather than scholarly research. Conversely, DuBois' work showed that the Negro's role in Reconstruction was not one of ineptitude nor corruption as writers such as Claude Bowers (*Tragic Era; The Revolution after Lincoln*); Edward A. Pollard (*The Lost Cause Regained*); and others had claimed. On the other hand, the African slave trade was the subject of his doctoral dissertation which was published in 1896 as the first volume of the new Harvard Historical Studies series under the title *The Suppression of the African Slave Trade*. This work was acclaimed to be the "first scientific historical work" written by a Negro.

Yet, it was DuBois' *The Souls of Black Folk* (1903), which set forth his personal pro-black attitudes and principles. This volume of essays was considered "dangerous for Negroes to read" by at least two southern newspaper editors.[5] This volume's uncompromising demand was for blacks to be accorded the rights the world recognized for all men. This included DuBois' rejection of Booker T. Washington's flattery and accommodationist approach toward the white South. Thus, it is understandable why many white southerners found *The Souls of Black Folk* dangerous reading for Negroes. It challenged all of the sub-human theses about the Negro that were all too frequently circulated throughout the South.

Another important intellectual who contributed to the black response to the racist propaganda was Carter G. Woodson. Woodson earned a Ph.D. degree from Harvard in 1912. He devoted his life to the study of the Negro as a participant in the making of history. To this end, he established the Association for the Study of Negro Life and History in 1915. One year later, he founded the quarterly, *Journal of Negro History.* He served as editor of this publication until his death in 1950. Furthermore, in 1926 he organized the first annual Negro History Week.

Woodson, unlike DuBois, was not a political activist. Instead, he focused his attention upon educating blacks and whites in an innovative way that would prevent a recurrence of past mistakes. To accomplish this he believed blacks had to be pioneers in developing a more desirable education. He wrote:

Negroes who have been so long inconvenienced and denied opportunities for development are naturally afraid of anything that sounds like discrimination. They are anxious to have everything the white man has even if it is harmful. The possibility of originality in the Negro, therefore, is discounted one hundred percent to maintain a nominal equality. If the whites decide to take up Mormonism the Negroes must follow their lead. If the whites neglect such a study, then the Negroes must do likewise. The author, however, does not have such an attitude. He considers the educational system as it has developed both in Europe and America an antiquated process which does not hit the mark even in the case of the needs of the white man himself. If the white man wants to hold on to it, let him do so; but the Negro, so far as he is able, should develop and carry out a program of his own.[6]

He contended that American education was a problem for the Negro because it taught him to hate his own history. For example Woodson wrote:

The "educated Negroes" have the attitude of contempt toward their own people because in their own as well as in their mixed schools Negroes are taught to admire the Hebrew, the Greek, the Latin and the Teuton and to despise the African.[7]

Such teachings in Woodson's view did not aid the black man, but handicapped him. The more educated such a student became, the more estranged he was in his thinking toward his own people. Woodson cited an example of this estrangement when a Negro Doctor of Philosophy was asked to teach a new course on the Negro. The faculty member replied, "he knew nothing about the Negro. He did not go to school to waste his time that way."[8]

For example, Woodson cited the purposeful omission of Africa in history by stating the accomplishments that came from the so-called "dark" continent.

You would never thereby learn that Africans first domesticated the sheep, goat, and cow, developed the idea of trial by jury, produced the first stringed instruments, and gave the world its greatest boon in the discovery of iron. You would never know that prior to the Mohammedan [sic] invasion about 1000 A.D. these natives in the heart of Africa had developed powerful kingdoms which were later organized as the Songhay Empire on the order of that of the Romans and boasting of similar grandeur.[9]

This educational program that the Negro should have according to Woodson should contain a knowledge of self. It was for this reason that he devoted his life to studying Negro history.

Woodson's contributions refuted the negative portrayals of Dixon and Page. African civilization was given a more accurate treatment than the emotional, biased renditions of these anti-black propagandists.

In addition, Woodson filled in the missing gaps in American education. The conspicuous silence on the Negro's accomplishments were filled by this African American historian's invaluable research.

Less well known than DuBois or Woodson, but more direct in his reaction to the anti-black propagandists was Sutton E. Griggs. He grew up during the period of the racist literary assault. He challenged these anti-Negro portrayals, including the characterization of the loud, semi-literate black preacher. Both his writings and his career helped to affirm the black man's humanity and worth at a time when he was being attacked by fictional pseudo-scientific literature.

Sutton Elbert Griggs was born in 1872 in Chatfield, Texas. He was the son of a Baptist clergyman, Allen R. Griggs. This fact undoubtedly influenced young Sutton's education. He went through the public schools of Dallas. After completing the course of study there, he enrolled in Bishop College, which was then located in Marshall, Texas. In 1890 he graduated from that institution. He continued his education in preparation for a ministerial career at the Richmond Theological Seminary (now Virginia Union University) in Richmond, Virginia, from 1890 to 1893.

Griggs' career as a clergyman was launched soon after his graduation from the Richmond Theological Seminary. He was called to his first pastorate in Berkley, Virginia, where he stayed for two years.[10] The young clergyman then moved to Tennessee where he served the First Baptist Church of East Nashville. He remained there until 1913 at which time he assumed the pastorate of the Tabernacle Baptist Church of Memphis, Tennessee.

The youthful minister began his literary career almost simultaneously with his duties as a cleric. His first book, *Imperium in Imperio* was published in 1899. Quickly following on a regular schedule were four more novels which concluded in 1908 with *Pointing the Way*. A close analysis will show that these fictional works defended the black American's basic rights, including the right to vote.

It is certainly clear that the primary motivation for the young author was his sincere desire to rebut the distortions presented by Page, Dixon, and others. He mentioned specifically in several writings the "Reverend Thomas Dixon, Jr." by name. In *The Hindered Hand; or The Reign of the Repressionist*, this defender of African American interests included a postscript to the novel subtitled "A Hindering Hand."[11] In this appendix, Griggs with a direct personal attack refuted the positions of Dixon's writings. Likewise, Griggs reacted just as strongly against Dixon in his political and social treatise, *The One Great Question, A Study of Southern Conditions at Close Range* (1907). In that work, Griggs wrote:

> The better element of the white south spews the Rev. Thomas Dixon, Jr., and his grossly misleading productions, out of its mouth, but his adroit groupings of half truths which make abominable untruths are but the legitimate fruit of a system of repression, a system repugnant to the moral sense of civilization.[12]

Thus, Griggs simply dismissed Dixon's writings as unworthy of the better element of the white South's reading audience. Such a refutation of a highly influential white southerner during this period was extremely rare. Thus, it can easily be seen why young Griggs was dubbed militant by many of his contemporaries, as well as by later scholars.[13]

Despite his degree of militancy, if Griggs saw something in an adversary's writing with which he agreed, he was not opposed to echoing its pronouncements. It is quite obvious that he was influenced by Thomas

Nelson Page's call for a biracial search for commonality as a solution to the South's race question. In 1904 Page wrote:

> A possible step in reaching the solution of the question might be for a reasonably limited number of representative Southern men to meet in conference a reasonable number of those colored men of the South who are more familiar with actual conditions there, and thus are representative of the most enlightened and experienced portion of that race. These, in a spirit of kindness and of justice, might confer together and try to find some common ground on which both shall stand and formulate some common measures as to which both sides shall agree and which both shall advocate.[14]

Three years later, Griggs wrote:

> There are men in the South among both whites and colored able to speak to the minds and hearts of the people; such men among the negroes as Prof. W. E. B. DuBois and among the whites as W. H. Fleming and E. Gardner Murphy, together with others in both races.[15]

It is extremely unlikely that the similarity of these two statements was coincidental. Although Griggs made no reference to Page's earlier pronouncement, it is almost certain he was familiar with his adversary's publication.

Consequently it would appear that Griggs, while rebuffing the literature of the anti-black propagandists, found some statements with which his ideas coincided. However, it would appear that the agreement was rare. Indeed, it should be clearly understood that Griggs had far more differences (which he pointed out) with the anti-black propagandists than agreements.

Griggs in one sense was not unique. He was part of a larger black response to racism. The response included "grass roots" protesters, as well as intellectuals. It included such elements as the Woman's Department of the National Baptist Convention and advocates for a black owned and controlled Baptist Publishing House.

However, the black response certainly was aided by a movement of black intellectual scholarship that predated the famed Harlem Renaissance of the 1920s. This earlier movement attempted to stymie the negative portrayals of African history. Such scholars as DuBois and Woodson wrote of the black man's participation and contributions to world civilization. They became the penmen for a new black spirit that was attempting to assert its own independent interpretation of historical events. They cast black life in far more favorable light than had previously been done.

While Griggs was certainly part of this black response movement, he also was unique. Griggs more than any other black writer launched personal attacks upon his intended targets. Particularly, he aimed his writings against the prolific venom that came from Thomas Dixon's pen.

Needless to say, for an African American to engage in the type of writings that Sutton E. Griggs did required courage. Griggs wrote his African American apologetics during an era in which intolerance, economic intimidation, and physical violence against blacks were every day occurrences in the South. Furthermore, Griggs was not domiciled in the North nor a foreign country when he wrote his pro-black literature. While he was publishing a steady flow of books sympathetic to the black southerner, he lived in Virginia and Tennessee.

Indeed, this valiant early defender of African American rights put forth theological and sociological thoughts that challenged the status quo of his day. To understand Griggs' thinking, we must delve deeper into his life's story.

NOTES

[1]This was the consensus of most Europeans after they encountered Africans according to Winthrop D. Jordan, *White Over Black: American Attitudes Toward the Negro, 1550-1812* (Baltimore: Penguin Books, Inc., 1969), pp. 7-11. The need to refute the anti-black propagandists of the late nineteenth and early twentieth centuries was not the first stimulus for African American literary achievement. Even under the yoke of slavery, there were some literary productions by black Americans at least a century before Dixon and Page's attacks. As early as 1761, Jupiter Hammon published his poem, "An Evening Thought, Salvation by Christ, with Penitential Cries." Almost a decade later, the famed Phillis Wheatley published her first poem, "On the death of the Reverend George Whitefield." Although neither of these poems set forth any racial positions, they do of themselves demonstrate that blacks were capable of producing serious literature even under the most undesirable circumstances.

[2]This practice has lasted until the present. Amos Jones, Director of Christian Education for the National Baptist Convention, U.S.A., Inc.'s Publishing House in Nashville, Tennessee said approximately only 20% of the churches in the Convention use their literature, Speech, Memphis Baptist Ministers Association, Memphis, Tennessee, Pentecostal Baptist Church, May 30, 1989.

[3]Leroy Fitts, *A History of Black Baptists* (Nashville: Broadman Press, 1985) pp. 84-85.

[4]*Journal of the Thirty-fifth Annual Session of the National Baptist Convention*, (Chicago, September, 1915), p. 235.

[5]Saunders Redding, "Introduction", in *The Souls of Black Folk* by W. E. Burghardt DuBois (Greenwich, Conn.: Fawcett Publications, Inc., 1961) p. x.

[6]Carter Godwin Woodson, *The Mis-Education of the Negro* (Revised ed.; Washington: The Associated Publishers, Inc., 1977) pp. xi-xii.

[7]*Ibid.*, p. 1.

[8]*Ibid.*

[9]*Ibid.*, pp. 21-22.

[10]"Called" here refers to the Baptist Church's doctrine of congregational election of its pastors.

[11]Sutton E. Griggs, *The Hindered Hand; or the Reign of the Repressionist* (3rd ed.; New York: A M S Press, 1969).

[12]Sutton E. Griggs, *The One Great Question, a Study of Southern Conditions at Close Range* (Philadelphia: Orion Publishing Co., 1907), p. 52.

[13]The studies that have been done on Sutton E. Griggs have only looked at him as a novelist. Among the three articles written on Griggs there has been disagreement over the degree of his militancy. Hugh Gloster's, "Sutton E. Griggs: Novelist of the New Negro," *Phylon* IV (fourth quarter, 1943), 335-345, saw Griggs as a prototype of a new militancy among black writers. On the other hand, Robert A. Bone's, *The Negro Novel in America* (Revised ed.; New Haven and London, 1965), pp. 32-33 saw Griggs as being ambivalent in his stance. Bone seems to equate Griggs' militancy to his view of violence. Since Griggs was clearly nonviolent in all of his works, Bone questions if Gloster is correct in his

evaluation of Griggs' militancy. The third article is by Robert E. Fleming, "Sutton E. Griggs: Militant Black Novelist," *Phylon* XXXIV (March, 1973), 73-77. Fleming sees Griggs as a militant for his time. He says it is the devices used and the style of Griggs' writing which makes him militant and not the issue of violence.

[14]Thomas Nelson Page, *The Negro: the Southerner's Problem* (New York: C. Scribner's sons, 1904) p. 161.

[15]Griggs, *The One Great Question*, p. 56.

CHAPTER III

Biographical Briefs

Biographical data on Sutton Griggs is very meager. In all of Griggs' publications he made few references to his personal life's story. Only in isolated pockets are there bits of his vita recorded. None of these recordings is in depth or fully revealing about the personal side of the man. Thus, from short fragmented references we shall endeavor to present the relevant aspects of his life that cast light upon his ideas for racial healing.

It is clear that one of the most profound influences upon the proponent of social efficiency was his father, the Reverend Allen R. Griggs, Sr. The elder Griggs had been a slave in Georgia.[1] From such a deprived status the father rose to become a pioneer in black Baptist beginnings in Texas. Although initially A. R. Griggs was ill-equipped educationally, he was a progressive minded individual who took advantage of every learning opportunity afforded him. Sutton gave the following narration of his father's educational strivings:

> When my father was a lad there was a stray dog that had the habit of sucking eggs that belonged to a Mrs. Andrews, a white woman of Texas. She told my father that she would teach him his alphabet if he would kill that dog. He crawled under the house and put an end to his career. Mrs. Andrews taught him his alphabet. Later he organized and erected houses of worship for five hundred churches, established the first colored high school and the first colored newspaper in Texas, and took the lead in founding four colleges. He was instrumental in bringing about co-operation between the white and colored Baptists of Texas. He was a great factor in the founding of the American Baptist Theological Seminary.[2]

This is a lucid description of the son's respect and admiration for his father. Although Sutton studied Charles Darwin, Thomas Huxley, Benjamin Kidd, and others, it is apparent that the earliest and most profound influence upon him was his father.

As Sutton stated, the elder Griggs was instrumental in the genesis of the American Baptist Theological Seminary. He worked in close harmony with his son in getting this project started. It was the father who took over most of the duties of the National Baptist Convention's Educational Committee so Sutton could be free to launch his efforts behind the formation of the Nashville school. Regularly the father substituted for the son at the Convention by the submission of the Committee's reports.[3]

Further evidence of the close bond between father and son can be seen in the later vita of Sutton. After encountering disappointment and failure in Memphis, (which shall shortly be detailed) he returned to Denison, Texas, where he assumed the pastorate of a congregation that the elder Griggs had once served. In light of black Baptist traditions,[4] it is

Figure 2. Reverend A. R. Griggs, Sr.

safe to infer that the congregation's acceptance of the son meant the younger man had many of the qualities of his father.

In addition, to his paternal ancestor, Sutton Griggs enjoyed an harmonious relationship with other family members. It was during his first pastorate in Berkley, Virginia that he married Emma J. Williams of Portsmouth, Virginia, on May 10, 1897.[5] Although *The Dictionary of American Negro Biography* records "a childless union...lasted until his death,"[6] the *Pittsburgh Courier* reported he had an adopted daughter, Eunice Griggs.[7] Also, the same paper revealed that he had a brother, Allen Griggs, Jr.

Although intimate information is nonexistent, we can determine that Sutton and Emma had a compatible life together. Her high opinion of her spouse was reflected in her efforts to preserve his memory in Memphis following his death. In 1937, T. O. Fuller reported that Emma was "endeavoring to perpetuate her late husband's name by the establishment of 'Griggs Institute' at Memphis."[8]

Furthermore, from Griggs' own account his wife was supportive of his ventures. In reference to his economic woes, Griggs called his spouse "the companion of my struggles, and my fellow sufferer..."[9] Such descriptive terms suggest that despite the external pressures, the couple's marriage was cemented "for richer or poorer."

The changes in Griggs' life were not just limited to his publications. Reflections of the metamorphosis were seen in the shift of his involvement in organizations that addressed the issue of racial equality. While in Nashville, Sutton Griggs was an active part of the country's college-educated professional men who composed the Niagara Movement's members.[10] However, when the Niagara Movement's scion, the National Association for the Advancement of Colored People, received an application for a Memphis branch in 1917 Griggs' name was missing from the petition.[11] This was merely a biographical consistency with the ideological drift that Griggs had with W. E. B. DuBois, who was instrumental in both the Niagara Movement and the NAACP. At least on this point, we see Griggs' actions and publications as being consistent.

Finances were a problem for Sutton Griggs. The root of his personal monetary woes was the cost of his extensive publications.Griggs published and distributed all of his writings himself. This gave him a limited market for his literary productions. According to him, the only sales that his books netted were those generated by personal contact.[12] As a result, Griggs dubbed his first six books financial failures.[13] The fourth book *The Hindered Hand*, particularly was a bitter disappointment for the author.

According to Griggs, this book was produced as a response to the unanimous action taken by the National Baptist Convention at a meeting in Philadelphia, Pennsylvania, in 1903. There the convention voted that Griggs "should make suitable answer to the tirades of the Rev. Mr. Dixon."[14] With this backing from the Convention, the writer set up a corporation and sold stock in it to investors. He persuaded his backers with the endorsement of the Convention's 17,200 congregations, and 2,500,000 members.[15] Unfortunately, the promised support from the religious body never materialized, and *The Hindered Hand*, printed in 1905 followed the same course of failure that his earlier publications had taken.

Not only had the Convention's vocal support caused others to invest in Griggs' corporation, but it also caused him a personal financial reversal of unprecedented proportions. In this enterprise, Griggs said, "I waded out as never before, utilizing practically all the cash and credit that I had in the venture."[16]

From this point forward the author/publisher continued to dig an economic hole for himself in an attempt to climb out of financial failure. Finally, with his publication of *Wisdom's Call* in 1911, Griggs was surprised by "the character of the impression made by the book..."[17] This work not only attracted the attention of a limited black clientele, but northern and southern whites as well. Favorable reviews of the book came from white southern politicians and civic leaders, as well as northern newspapers like *The Chicago Record-Herald*.[18]

Under the auspices of the Southern Baptist Convention's Home Mission Board, an attempt was made "to bring the white ministers of the South to a clearer understanding of the proper race relationship in the South."[19] *Wisdom's Call* interested V. I. Masters, the Editorial Secretary of the Home Mission Board, because of its posture of advocating a mutual "live and let live" southern racial policy.

Despite the white response to *Wisdom's Call*, Griggs said it followed the same course of failure as did the preceding six publications. Out of disappointment Griggs laid the blame for this latest failure upon his people. With the endorsement of southern whites, Griggs, now felt this climate of acceptability for his works provided southern Negroes with no viable excuse to avoid buying his publications. Yet, they still only bought it when confronted personally by the peddling writer.

Undoubtedly, the acceptance of his writings by southern whites, albeit in small numbers, had some impact upon the future course of his writings. Whether out of economic necessity, moderation in ideals, or both, Griggs clearly moved ahead in his philosophy of social efficiency. After the publication of *Wisdom's Call*, Griggs began to advocate interracial cooperation. His epoch of protest had now been abandoned in favor of an open advocacy of mutual co-operation between the two races. He put the brunt of the burden of this co-operation upon the Negro. Repeatedly throughout the remainder of his career, Griggs counselled the African American that he had to impress others favorably. For example, he said:

> The Negroes may build churches, establish schools, operate fraternal organizations, buy homes and manifest every other sign of progress, but unless they pay attention to the matter of the world's opinion concerning themselves, they will find their good name as a race steadily sinking as they rise, and all of their advancement will not be compensation for the sorrowful existence that they shall be called upon to lead.[20]

Consistently, from this point until the end of his life, Griggs espoused the view that the black man was dependent upon the way others perceived him. The tone of Griggs' later publications were imbued with this theme. Based upon his own narration in *The Story of My Struggles*, and the comments of his close friend T. O. Fuller, economics played a big role in this transition.

In addition to his experience with his publications, it is most evident that his involvement in the founding of the American Baptist Seminary was instrumental in shaping his thinking. This venture enabled Griggs to see his theoretical views of interracial cooperation materialize into reality. It was through his appeals to the Southern Baptist Convention that a supporting partnership was formed with the National Baptist Convention. Together a biracial Baptist support mechanism was formed for the founding and continuing sustenance of the Nashville school. Griggs had a rare opportunity for an African American when he first addressed the Southern Baptist Convention in St. Louis, Missouri, in May 1913. Although some scholars have cast doubt upon Griggs' persuasive speaking abilities in attracting white support,[21] it was after his address that the Southern Baptists chose to join a cooperative effort in support of the American Baptist Seminary. The importance that Griggs played in the

Figure 3. Griggs Hall

school's establishment can be seen in the fact that Sutton and his father had a building on the campus named after them.

Like his prototype, Booker T. Washington, Griggs saw that it was possible to win white cooperation for enterprises that benefited African Americans. Thus, after the Southern Baptists' endorsement in 1913, Griggs pursued with vigor the cause that had brought him some measure of success.

Griggs remained devoted to the Nashville school even after he moved to Memphis. At what had to be a great personal sacrifice, he even commuted between Memphis and Nashville while serving as president of the American Baptist Theological Seminary during 1925 and 1926. Apparently, the sole factor in accepting this position was his strong desire to have an educated African American clergy.

As noble as his work with the Seminary was, his most memorable labors outside of writing was his pastorate of the Tabernacle Baptist Church of Memphis. From the date of his installation as pastor of the church, Griggs received a favorable acceptance from both black and white officials in Memphis. The installation sermon was preached by T. O. Fuller, who was president of Howe Institute, the black Baptist School in Memphis. *The Commercial Appeal* stated that Griggs was "declared to be a recognized man of his race."[22]

With such a favorable reception, Griggs proved himself to be a man of vision and leadership whose influence far exceeded the confines of his congregation. Located on Turley Street when Griggs was initially called as pastor, it was not long before Griggs had the church engaged in a building program at a new address on Lauderdale Street. Construction

Figure 4. Tabernacle Baptist Church

had begun on the new facilities for Tabernacle as early as April 1916.[23] The new structure was an extraordinary undertaking for an African American congregation of that period. The new church was envisioned to be an institutional church that would do more than provide the traditional Sunday School and preaching service. The plans called for Tabernacle to have a gymnasium, swimming pool, and an employment bureau. These facilities were intended to lure "young men away from low pool rooms and other places of vice."[24]

Following the example of Booker T. Washington in establishing Tuskegee Institute in a hostile white environment, Griggs assured white Memphians that the church's ministry would benefit them as well. One of the goals of the institutional church was to be the teaching of Negro women "domestic science so as to increase their efficiency as cooks for white people."[25] Such a statement of purpose showed that though the church facility was unconventional for blacks, it nevertheless was to be a conservative ministry that posed no threat to the white supremacist status quo.

From the church base, Griggs projected his influence in other areas in the society. Among the activities that he undertook was the founding of The Public Welfare League. This organization published all of his writings after he became domiciled in Memphis. The purpose of The Public Welfare League was to pursue intraracial co-operation. Griggs outlined the goals of the group in the following manner:

1. To afford an opportunity for the development of Negro talent.
2. To build up Negro enterprises, and Negro professional life, for the good of all.
3. To give to each member of the race who is trying to rise the help of all, thus setting forth the value of co-operation.
4. To shape a friendly public sentiment toward the Negro race in the minds of all men.

5. To collectively watch out for the interests of the race at all points, and answer every call for help.[26]

Although number four is a subscription to interracial co-operation, the elevation of the African American through racial solidarity was the ultimate purpose. In fact, the organization seems to have been an attempt to synthesize DuBois' Talented Tenth with Washington's National Negro Business League. Number one while not numerically limiting black talent as DuBois' Talented Tenth doctrine had done, it still displayed shades of DuBois' belief that black talents should have opportunities to develop. On the other hand, number two reflects Washington's teachings on the merits of black entrepreneurship and land ownership.

In an effort to elevate the state of the African American, Griggs sought to organize neighborhood improvement societies[27] during the mid teens of the twentieth century. Apparently, the purpose of these societies was to stress citizenship among blacks. Such societies undoubtedly were envisioned by Griggs as a stabilizing force in the African American Community. However, if any of these planned societies became operational, then their work was not publicized as there is no later reference to them.

Similar in intent, Griggs worked for the introduction of textbooks in the school system that would "stress the points needed for the civic education of negroes...."[28] To this end, Griggs secured the support of the superintendent of the Memphis City Schools, A. A. Kincannon. Working with Griggs in this venture was William N. Jones, a black social service employee with the city.

Jones was not a token black, who publicly supported Griggs' work. The record supports this conclusion. It was reported that:

> The Negro Baptist Ministers' Alliance, through its religious and civic committee are said to have placarded tributes paid Dr. Griggs by psychologists and sociologists who in themselves are "stars of the first magnitude," among whom are Hon. George R. James, member of the federal reserve board, Memphis and Dr. C. V. Ronian, author of "The Negro and American Civilization," Nashville.[29]

The Baptist Minister's Alliance at the time was the largest and most influential professional group of black clergy in Memphis. Thus, despite Griggs' overtures toward interracial cooperation, he still enjoyed the support of his colleagues in the ministry.

There were other sources of endorsements for Griggs from blacks. In fact, he even attracted financial support from influential members of the race. For example, Charles Banks, vice president of the National Negro Business League, voluntarily contributed $100 to Tabernacle's building program.[30] Apparently, he was impressed with the church's multi-ministry approach in serving the African American Community.

In addition to his own race, Griggs won the support of many influential white southerners. His accommodationist appeals found an audience among whites, who relished Griggs' compromising statements. *The Commercial Appeal* even saw fit to publicize Griggs' book, *Paths of*

Progress, when it came off the press in 1925 accompanied by a conciliatory statement from the author. In the article, Griggs said the book's goal was:

...for the colored people of the United States to understand the manner in which the race problem must be solved, the races must work out the problem without federal aid or interference...Colored people and Northern whites must get a firmer grip on this fact.[31]

Such a statement was readily received by the white South who continued to complain about outside interference during the years following the Civil War through the Civil Rights era. The doctrine of "state's rights" and the sovereignty of the South were compatible with the announcement made by Griggs.

Following World War I, a northern labor shortage brought recruiters to the South in an attempt to persuade black laborers to relocate to the North. This labor shortage resulted from a virtual halt of European immigration during the war. This condition was further aggravated by an exodus of some immigrants who already were in America. In December 1919, the *Memphis Chamber of Commerce Journal* reported that approximately 80 Italians were leaving Detroit daily in order to return to their homeland.[32]

Coincident with this was the mass exodus of southern African Americans for the promising enticements of northern industry. The migration became so extensive that the Memphis Chamber of Commerce created the Industrial Welfare Committee in 1919. It was recorded that the committee was going to cooperate "with the negroes by matching dollars in order that institutions of this character may be fostered."[33] The institutions had to have a character that met the broad based concerns of blacks. Furthermore the institutions that received matching funds from the Industrial Welfare Committee had to be doing something to help themselves. In the latter regard, the committee remained adamant in this position throughout its reports. For example, in 1921 the Committee's chairman, George R. James, reported:

The Committee has rigidly adhered to its policy to expend no moneys for promotion or maintenance, but has confined its disbursements to the paying for equipment for such undertakings as have been postured and maintained by the negroes themselves.[34]

Thus, it is clear that while this committee was charged with getting results that would entice blacks to stay in the "Bluff City," it was not given authority to aid any organization that was not already doing something to address the grievances of Memphis' black citizens.

Apparently, among the recipients of the Committee's disbursements, Tabernacle Baptist Church was doing a superior job of meeting the committee's requirements. The April 15, 1921 report showed Tabernacle having received $6,185.25, while the next highest beneficiary netted only $399.93.[35]

There are two justifiable explanations that come to mind as to why

Tabernacle received such a disproportionate share of the Committee's grants. First, Pastor Griggs throughout his career had never advocated black migration from the South. His later writings openly advised against it. On the other hand, the earlier writings assumed the South would be the home of the majority of African Americans. In these early writings, Griggs constantly argued for better treatment of the Negro in the South. Nowhere did he ever suggest wholesale removal from the former Confederacy. Thus, the stance of Griggs on this issue was consistent with the desired goals of the Industrial Welfare Committee.

Secondly, Tabernacle was in a position to attract such a large payment because it was unique among the institutions for African Americans in Memphis. One of the complaints lodged by blacks was the dearth of park and recreational facilities for their race. Tabernacle, with its gymnasium and swimming pool, helped to meet this need. Thus, a $6,185.25 grant to the church was more economical for the Chamber than undertaking a completely new facility in the vicinity of Tabernacle.

Griggs at the height of his pastorate in Memphis attracted both black and white support from the city's prominent businessmen. Such a coalition enabled the clergyman to launch a planned weekly paper entitled *The Neighbor*. In December 1919, it was announced that twenty-five thousand copies of the publication would be distributed without charge. This magnanimous gesture was "made possible by the co-operation of leading negro business men, a number of firms owned by white people and a committee of the Memphis Chamber of Commerce."[36]

The author's plan was to distribute special issues of *The Neighbor* in every southern city that had a substantial African American population. The name of the publication demonstrated its intent. It was disclosed that the paper's goal was to echo the progress of southern race relations. *The Commercial Appeal* reported the new issue's comprehensive ambitions.

> The purpose of the publication is to demonstrate the progress being made by Memphis negroes and to call attention to opportunities for greater development. The paper will seek to give wholesome counsel as to the best way for the members of the race to deal with their problems as they arise.[37]

This description could have represented most of Griggs' publications. Thus, *The Neighbor* was not designed to bring any new message so far as Griggs' philosophy was concerned. Consequently, there is no evidence that Griggs compromised any of his ideas to cater to a specific segment of his supporters through this medium.

During his tenure at Tabernacle, Griggs was known far and wide for his philosophy of social efficiency. His influence extended beyond the "Bluff City" and the core of black businessmen and Chamber of Commerce supporters that he had there. In 1925 the American Woodman, at the time America's strongest black fraternal organization, voted at a session held in Denver, Colorado "to adopt the philosophy of racial advancement as worked out by Dr. Sutton E. Griggs in his books 'Guide to Racial Greatness' and 'Stepping Stones to Higher Things.' "[38]

Later, in the same year the African American clergy of St. Louis aligned themselves with Sutton Griggs' philosophy of social efficiency. *The Commercial Appeal* reported that the Missouri group "passed strong resolutions endorsing the leadership of Dr. Sutton E. Griggs and pledging to join in his programme for the social reconstruction of the race."[39]

In the following year, *The Commercial Appeal* announced that within Tennessee, the two most recognizable institutions of higher learning for African Americans, Fisk University and A & I College of Nashville gave "hearty approval" for Griggs' system of socialization.[40] It was also stated that an educational conference would later follow with the intention of "devising a way for the negro children to get the full benefit of the system which Dr. Griggs has wrought out for their good."[41]

The concept of an institutional church found audiences in other cities for Griggs. Within three years after coming to Tabernacle, he was invited to Knoxville and Springfield, Missouri, to impart information on this concept. Furthermore, it was revealed that the idea of an institutional church was producing a co-operative effort in those communities between white people and black churches.[42] Thus, Griggs' efforts in Memphis became a kind of pattern after which other southern societies planned developments.

It should also be mentioned that Sutton E. Griggs was not only winning a following for his ideas away from Tabernacle but there as well. Based on an announcement that "The Kingdom Builders" class would meet at the church on a Sunday afternoon, we can infer that the congregation accepted their pastor's doctrines.[43] Griggs persistently lobbied the Sunday School Board of the National Baptist Convention to accept his publication, *Kingdom Builder's Manual* as a textbook. This never materialized. However, within his own congregation there was a class named after the text.

Thus, on the surface, Griggs' career at Tabernacle looked impressive. He was finally making an impact that stretched beyond the confines of his race, vicinity, and denomination. Endorsements for his labors reached an all time high. He enjoyed the backing of prominent citizens of both races. Institutional subscriptions to his philosophy were increasing at a steady pace.

Despite the superficial appearance, the truth was this was a beguiling age for Sutton E. Griggs. By 1925 Griggs had incurred a group of critics to accompany his supporters. The voices of discontent began to take their toll upon the energetic author.[44] Many of his writings took on a defensive posture such as that found in *Paths of Progress*. Furthermore, Griggs' labors required a substantial amount of travel. Speaking engagements, book promotions, and his labors with the National Baptist Convention took him away from his full-time institutional church more than was advisable. Looming beyond the deceptive age of the decade of the twenties was the disastrous thirties.

The stock market crash of October 1929 soon plunged the country into the Great Depression. An already fragile economy within black America had no defenses for such a financial catastrophe. Many large black congregations soon found themselves in a position of insolvency within months after the crash. During the first eighteen months of the thirties, the *Pittsburgh Courier* regularly reported on black churches across America that were hopelessly in debt. The articles stated they were either in danger of foreclosure or were auctioned off to the highest bidder. These congregations ranged from St. Louis to Washington, D.C. in the eastern belt, where the majority of African Americans lived in that era.

Unfortunately, Tabernacle became a victim of this trend. On Monday morning, October 30, 1930, Tabernacle was sold at public auction for $15,000 to satisfy a mortgage that the Universal Life Insurance Company held on the property.[45] The congregation had attempted to "stay" the auction, but their efforts were in vain.

Such a fate for the church meant the end of Griggs' pastorate in Memphis. Disgraced, the clergyman moved to Texas where (as has been already mentioned) he assumed the pastorate of the Hopewell Baptist Church in Denison. Griggs remained there until the latter part of 1932, when he resigned to begin a Baptist supported religious and civic affairs institute in Houston.[46]

Unfortunately, Griggs did not long survive this latest venture. Within a month of his arrival in Houston, the social crusader died. Suddenly the earthly sojourn of the philosopher theologian came to a halt on Monday, January 2, 1933, in Houston. He was buried there on January 5, 1933.

Following the loss of their edifice and pastor, Tabernacle rebounded. The congregation began holding its worship services at the chapel of the Roger Williams-Howe Institute at the corner of Wellington and St. Paul Streets.[47] In an attempt to quickly put the unpleasant past behind it, Tabernacle in advertising its Homecoming Celebration in 1931, flaunted in the headlines its new pastor, William G. Walker, and the fact that the program was not a financial rally. To further distance themselves from the Griggs era, the announcement said "New Members are coming to us now that we have a new pastor, Rev. Wm. G. Walker."[48]

Steadily fortunes improved for Tabernacle. It eventually purchased an edifice on Kendale Avenue that had previously belonged to an all white Presbyterian Congregation. The church still worships at that location.

The former site on Lauderdale was bought at the Auction by M. W. Bonner, who was the secretary of the Universal Life Insurance Company. Later, the property was sold to the developing and thriving Church of God in Christ. Temple Church of God in Christ is presently located at the address.

The disastrous end of Sutton Griggs in Memphis has overshadowed his contributions. As a clergyman and civic leader, Memphis has all but forgotten him. Serious scholarship, with the exception of David Tucker, has only considered his literary efforts. Even in this limited sphere the consideration has been even narrower, as only his novels have governed most of the attention.

Therefore, let us now turn our attention to an analysis of his early writings which challenged the theological and sociological status quo of the early twentieth century. There we find a clue as to what the young man believed, preached, and wrote.

NOTES

[1]David M. Tucker, *Black Pastors and Leaders: Memphis, 1819-1972* (Memphis: Memphis State University Press, 1975), p. 72.

[2]Sutton E. Griggs, *Paths of Progress; or Co-operation Between the Races, a Series of Addresses, Articles, and Essays* (Memphis: National Public Welfare League, 1925), p. 44.

[3]National Baptist Convention, *Journal of Thirty-Eighth Annual Session* (St. Louis, Mo., September 4-9, 1918), p. 249.

[4]In many African American Baptist Churches it has not been uncommon for a congregation to elect a pastor who is the son of a former pastor. Of course, this is predicated upon the son being an ordained clergyman. This practice is especially true where the father had been held in high regard and the son bears characteristics of his progenitor.

[5]Rayford W. Logan and Michael R. Winston eds., *Dictionary of American Negro Biography* (New York: W. W. Norton & Company, 1982, p. 271.

[6]*Ibid.*

[7]*Pittsburgh Courier*, Jan. 21, 1933, p. 10.

[8]T. O. Fuller, *History of the Negro Baptists of Tennessee* (Memphis: By author, 1936), p. 75.

[9]Sutton E. Griggs, *The Story of My Struggles* (Memphis: The National Public Welfare League, 1914), p. 14.

[10]August Meier, *Negro Thought in America, 1880-1915* (Ann Arbor: The University of Michigan Press, 1963), p. 180.

[11]The Memphis Branch National Association for the Advancement of Colored People Application for Charter, 1917. It should be noted that the absence of Griggs' name in and of itself is not evidence of a compromising posture. There were many African Americans who initially distrusted the NAACP because it was seen as an organization controlled by whites and elitist blacks. This perception was a major contributor to Marcus Garvey's appeal to a massive grass roots following.

[12]Griggs, *The Story of My Struggles*, 9. In addition to Griggs' book sales being limited because of his dependence upon personal contact, so was his influence. Although within scholarly circles Griggs attracted the attention of some of the country's most prestigious colleges and universities' faculty, for the most part his notoriety was regionally limited to the South; racially limited to blacks; and religiously limited to Baptists.

[13]*Ibid.*, 14.

[14]*Ibid.*, 12.

[15]*Ibid.*

[16]*Ibid.*, 13.

[17]*Ibid.*, 14.

[18]*Ibid.*, 15-16.

[19]*Ibid.*, 16.

[20]*Ibid.*, 20.

[21]David Tucker in *Black Pastors and Leaders*, p. 79 dismisses Griggs' oratorical and persuasive skills in winning white support in Memphis. Instead, Tucker asserts that Griggs received white support because he told blacks to stay in the South, which would insure an abundant cheap labor source for Dixie. Tucker has underestimated Griggs' persuasive appeal by failing to take into consideration that his endorsement from whites extended beyond Memphis and the South.

[22]*The Commercial Appeal*, April 13, 1913, p. 9.

[23]*Ibid.*, April 17, 1916, p. 5.

[24]*Ibid.*

[25]*Ibid.*

[26]Griggs, *The Story of My Struggles*, p. 24.

[27]*The Commercial Appeal*, July 9, 1916, p. 18.

[28]*Ibid.*

[29]*The Commercial Appeal*, March 30, 1924, p. 12.

[30]*Ibid.*, July 1, 1916, p. 8.

[31]This quote was printed in the News of "Bygone Days-50 Years Ago," *The Commercial Appeal*, August 20, 1975, p. 6.

[32]*Chamber of Commerce Journal*, II (December, 1919), p. 263.

[32]*Ibid.*

[34]*Memphis Chamber of Commerce Journal*, IV (May, 1921), p. 11.

[35]*Ibid.*

[36]*The Commercial Appeal*, Dec. 21, 1919, p. 15.

[37]*Ibid.*

[38]*Ibid.*, August 16, 1925, p. 14.

[39]*Ibid.*, December 15, 1925, p. 5.

[40]*Ibid.*, October 19, 1926, p. 8.

[41]*Ibid.*

[42]*Ibid.*, July 1, 1916, p. 8.

[43]*Ibid.*, August 16, 1925, p. 12.

[44]The voices of discontent for the most part were verbal. The one known exception was an article in the *Chicago Defender* by W. Allison Sweeney. Unfortunately, the issue of the *Defender* in which Sweeney's remarks were printed has been lost.

[45]*Pittsburgh Courier*, November 1, 1930, sec. 2, p. 1.

[46]Logan and Winston, 271.

[47]*Memphis World*, September 25, 1931, p. 3.

[48]*Ibid.*

CHAPTER IV

The Early Works

Sutton E. Griggs was both prolific and profound in his writings. Prior to 1913, the year he moved to Memphis, Griggs had written eight books. Five of these were novels. However, after their publication he abandoned fiction in favor of treatises that contained his theological and sociological thoughts, particularly as they applied to southern race relations.

Although the minister was a well-trained black cleric, his theology was not divorced from practical life. As has been the case with most African American theologians, his writings were not abstract, esoteric, or speculative.[1] Every volume he wrote had practical application to the Negro's struggle for equality and improvement. His religion was based on the realism of experience.

Consequently, it is impossible to separate his theological from his sociological concepts. One complements the other in an intertwining relationship. His theology was based upon his social concerns, and his sociological solutions to racism were governed by his theology.

The pre-Memphis Griggs was an energetic figure who pressed for equal treatment of blacks. He rejected all advocacy for racial discrimination whether it was based upon a distorted religious, pseudo-scientific, or biased argumentative hypothesis. According to Griggs, any debate for racial discrimination was unChristian, irrational, and unscientific.

Although not one of his pre-1913 books can be called a theological work, he still revealed some of his beliefs in his novels and treatises. It is critical to glean his theological thoughts in order to properly evaluate his positions and ideas and the causative forces that inspired them.

Griggs was an extremely complex man, especially so for the period and culture in which he lived. At a time when protestant fundamentalism was the norm throughout the Bible Belt, Griggs emerged as a believer in natural theology. That is, he relied more on reason as presented in nature than he did upon revelation. The complexity of his beliefs can be seen in his synthesis of Thomas Jefferson, Charles Darwin, and the Bible. All three of these sources greatly influenced young Griggs. Jefferson was repeatedly referred to as an authority on what was proper and just in both the fiction and nonfiction writings.

As a naturalist, Griggs believed Nature was as great a source of truth as there was. While Griggs believed in scripture and Divine revelation, he did not see them as independent of and superseding nature. The respect and belief that he had in the Bible can be seen when he referred to it as the "earthly guide."[2] Yet, Griggs clearly was no Bible fanatic. His writings

did not constantly cite scripture after scripture as sources of his opinions. In *Wisdom's Call,* for example, the scriptures are never cited as the
inspiration for his thinking.[3] Rather, the various passages which are mentioned serve only to substantiate his thinking. In essence, Griggs saw the
scriptures as a tool to be used in gauging whether or not one's reasoning
was valid.

In his praise of the British theologian and biologist, Henry Drummond,
Griggs wrote:

> Soon the world heard his [Drummond's] voice proclaiming in the tone of
> one speaking with authority that the new revelations of science contained
> no poison for Christianity; that the new teacher, nature, was the friend, not
> the enemy, of the old teacher, the Bible. He declared that Evolution and
> Christianity have the same author, 'the same end and the same spirit.'[4]

Griggs, like Drummond, believed that nature and Christianity were compatible. He did not believe that one had to choose between the new
scholarship of the late nineteenth century and Christian beliefs. In fact,
he saw these coalescing to form the whole truth.

The influence of Thomas Jefferson upon Griggs can be seen in his subscription to the belief in self-evident truths. Repeatedly throughout his
writings this naturalist theologian quoted from Jefferson's well-known
lines of the Declaration of Independence.

> We hold these truths to be self-evident, that all men are created equal, that
> they are endowed by their creator with certain unalienable rights; that
> among these are life, liberty and the pursuit of happiness.

To Griggs these words were as sacred as any of the scriptures. In his
mind, certain truths were obvious by nature.

In his treatise, *The One Great Question, a Study of Southern Conditions at Close Range*, Griggs cited many of the atrocities which were
committed against blacks.[5] In this work the literary crusader for black
justice merely presented the infractions which occurred. He presented
no scriptures nor theological arguments for fairness to the black southerner. It is obvious that he believed the morality and ethical propositions
of the issue were self-evident. Therefore, no elaborate defense of his
appeal for a redress of grievances was necessary. What was right was
obvious by nature.

This sense of the self-evidence of what was right, Griggs thought, was
the direction in which mankind was traveling. As man became more enlightened, Griggs thought it would become progressively more obvious
as to what was moral or immoral. In 1907 Griggs wrote:

> Again the moral sense of the world is and will continue to be opposed to the
> holding of a people back because of their color or race. Any section of the
> world that practices this will find itself out of tune with the enlightened
> sections of the human family.[6]

Discrimination and repression were immoral practices that were apparent to an enlightened individual. To Griggs, ethics were part of nature's
revelation. Therefore, the problem confronting society was not deter-

mining what was right but rather that of conforming to what was obviously right.

Foremost among the self-evident truths which nature had instituted was that of equality. So far as this doctrine was concerned, Jefferson definitely was the greatest influence upon him. Yet, he merged Biblical insights with Jefferson's views. In *Imperium in Imperio*, the fictional Bernard Belgrave, the President of the Imperium, speaks before that body in such a manner. Belgrave said:

> The Bible which the white people gave us, teaches us that we are men. The Declaration of Independence, which we behold them wearing over their hearts, tells us that all men are created equal. If as the Bible says, we are men; if, as Jefferson says, all men are equal; if, as he further states, governments derive all just powers from the consent of the governed, then it follows that the American government is in duty bound to seek to know our will as respects the laws and the men who are to govern us.[7]

Consequently, equality is a natural right which every citizen should expect of his government. Furthermore, both the Bible and the Declaration of Independence agree on this.

More examples of Griggs' synthesis of Christianity and natural rights being tantamount to equality can be found throughout his literature. In his sequel to *Unfettered, Dorlan's Plan*, he weaves together the new learning and orthodoxy when he states, "If God is represented as presiding over the forces of evolution, the Negro may claim that God and nature have fixed his status as a human being."[8] The message is that all men should be treated equally in their pursuit of their natural rights. This is a self-evident truth from God and nature.

According to Griggs this view is nothing new on his part. The self-evident right of equality goes back to the early framers of the new republic. The Constitution was formed in such a way that it followed the mold cast by the Declaration of Independence.[9] Griggs believed that implementation of such legal documents was the means to improved race relations.

In addition to equality, the young thinker believed that nature likewise endowed mankind with inherited traits. In addition to physical characteristics, Griggs believed behavior and personality were biologically inherited and not socially acquired. As a result, the inheritance theories of Griggs appear somewhat far fetched in light of the later corpus of knowledge.

He believed that the brutal and boorish characteristics of the human race were matters of inheritance. Such undesirable behavior was biologically transmitted from one generation to the next in his view. In *Wisdom's Call* he warned the white race against intermingling with those of their race who exhibited violent behavior. The warning stated:

> Such white men as brutalize their natures by their conduct toward Negroes must look to the white race for wives, and their offsprings are absorbed into the general body of the white race.... Is there anything more certain than,

37

that in due time a generation will arrive possessing in a marked degree a strain of brutality?[10]

In Griggs' opinion the white race at large would contribute to its degenerate state by becoming genetically linked to the lynchers and murderers who stalked the black man. Thus, what appeared to be a temporary victimization of the black man threatened the white race on a long term basis. If precaution was not used then the entire white race would become savage and uncivilized in the area of human relations.

More extensive use of the Naturalist's theory of inheritance was applied to the distinctions he saw among ethnic groups. It was by nature, in his view, that Asians and Africans were prone to accept unfaltering beliefs. On the other hand, the European was more probing and inquisitive than were either of the former two groups. Consequently, the European was more skeptical and less likely to accept information on its surface value.

The question thus emerges: if Griggs was correct in his assertions, why then was the white South so orthodox in its fundamental Christian beliefs? Needless to say, he had an answer. According to him, the reason for this was that Negro women told Bible stories to white youngsters.[11] Therefore, the cause of their orthodoxy resulted from the captivating, female Negro story-tellers. These women, by virtue of their nature to believe, told stories that were literal and devoid of interpretation or alteration.

It is evident that Griggs seriously subscribed to his theory of inherited human behavior. He particularly saw the class of poor whites as having been dominated by violent tendencies. He believed that even those who escaped the lower rung of the economic ladder still genetically had those base characteristics. Griggs stated:

Nathan Bedford Forrest hailed from this class, and as a result the American people have on their annals Fort Pillow and its savage-like massacre. When the war was over, the poor white class began to bestir itself in civil life, and from that class the nation derived the Hon. Benjamin R. Tillman, of South Carolina. And now literature is receiving its contribution from this class of whites, in the work being done by Mr. Thomas Dixon, Jr., of North Carolina, who does not hail from the more wealthy and more friendly element of Southern whites, but from mingling with the poorer classes, where hatred of the Negro was a part of the legacy handed down from parent to child.[12]

Thus, despite the notoriety of Tillman and Dixon, they could not divorce themselves from the dreaded inherited nature of bigotry and violence. It was their natural inheritance to assume the same ideas as their ancestors.

Griggs' belief in inherited character traits appeared to have been influenced by the new learning of the era. It is clear that the clergyman was a scholar who was well read in many fields. As a result, this influenced his theological perspective to be broad in its development. He was in touch with scientific and social theories, as well as having matriculated in theology.

These interdisciplinary studies were incorporated into Griggs' view of man, God, and man's ultimate destiny. For example, his view on inherited human behavior was admittedly influenced by the sociologist, Herbert Spencer.[13] In Dorlan's plan, Griggs quoted a passage from Spencer which he obviously held in high regard. "The emotional nature prompting the general mode of conduct is derived from ancestors—is a product of all ancestral activities."[14] Inheritance inundates any environmental influences upon changes or alterations in one's conduct.

It is indeed interesting that an evangelical Christian preacher had such a belief. After all, the evangelical message is that Jesus Christ can make new creatures out of his converts. There is no evidence in any of Griggs' writings which would support the opinion that he in any way subscribed to such an orthodox belief. In fact, the evidence supports the interpretation that Griggs believed the only way to alter human behavior was through selective breeding. This point will be discussed more completely later in this chapter.

In his political and social work, *The One Great Question, a Study of Southern Conditions at Close Range*, Griggs set forth a gloomy picture of human rights violations throughout the South. Illustrative of his mood was the similar comparison of horrors that he made of Nashville's County prison farm to that of Russia's Siberia.[14] Throughout the book, he spoke of atrocity after atrocity which were committed in Nashville and other southern communities against black citizens. Indeed, through all of Griggs' publications, it is clear he was displeased with the status quo on the sensitive issue of race relations.

Despite the mood of discontent and ugliness in his literature, Griggs was no pessimist. His view of history's course was not fatalistic in any way. He believed man had the potential and capacity to make conditions better. He did believe, however, that man could not make conditions better by himself. Rather, man's crusading efforts must be in harmony with nature's process of selection.

The complexity of this Christian preacher's theology can be seen in the fact that he synthesized natural rights of man, the Bible, and evolution into a theological position. Preaching and writing in a section of the country that eventually forced Charles Darwin's theory of evolution into court, Griggs openly embraced such ideas.[16] He readily quoted Thomas Huxley (one of Darwin's ardent supporters) and spoke admiringly of his scholarship.[17]

He wholeheartedly accepted Darwin's theory of natural selection of species. So far as Griggs was concerned, this was a self-evident truth which Darwin had adequately stated. In a confident manner he wrote of the theory as if it were law, not theory. In 1911 he penned the following:

> The scientists tell us that throughout the realm of nature there has been one long, continuous struggle for existence, that in this struggle the weak have gone to the wall, leaving the earth to those that proved to be the fittest to meet the condition that arose in the struggling. The species which now exist

were made strong by means of this crucial struggle for existence through which they have passed.[18]

There is no doubt that Griggs saw much merit in the evolutionary process of natural selection. Thus, it is easy to see how such theories influenced his ideas on how things could be improved for the future.

He believed that man could assist nature in its process of natural selection. According to Griggs, the way of making things better was simply to improve the human stock that was produced. Therefore, he advocated a system of selective breeding for mankind, whereby the "better element" of the white citizenry and the "worthy" Negroes would be preserved.[19] On the other hand, natural selection with assistance from the human element would eradicate the bad elements from the human race.[20]

Despite Griggs' advocacy for the preservation of the most desirable of both races, in none of his writings is there a hint of racial amalgamation. Apparently, a self-evident truth with him was a natural inclination to develop the best in each race without benefit of miscegenation.

Crucial to Griggs' belief in natural selection was the ultimate Darwinian doctrine of the survival of the fittest.[21] Griggs exposed his belief in the fittest as he repeatedly used such expressions as "the better element of the white South" and "worthy Negroes." In his opinion these groups composed those most fit for the acceptable social order.

One of the events which Griggs applauded as being a gathering of the most fit was when Fisk University's famed Jubilee Singers performed before Nashville's higher echelon of the white citizenry. In Griggs' view, the Jubilee Singers' music was contributing to a more advanced and fit society. On the other hand, he took a dim view of the popular ragtime music of the masses. He thought the latter contributed to the degeneracy of the listener. The following comparison clearly demonstrates his taste:

> The two cases are before us, the Negroes of the higher culture lending their talents to a noble cause and flooding a city of culture with delight, while the neglected Negroes are seen chasing the soothing classical music from the boards, interfering with the musical development of the country and giving to the nation a stimulant pronounced by an eminent scientist as baleful.[22]

The Naturalist Thinker was very pointed in his condemnation of the musical tastes of "neglected Negroes." Such comments were demonstrative that he felt the more noble elements of civilization should be concentrated upon intently. On the other hand, such debauchery as ragtime should be avoided.

As has been discussed in Chapter Two, Griggs thought that if race relations were to be improved it would have to be the fittest in both races who led the way. He believed the best blacks and whites would have to provide the leadership in order for their races to enter into a more harmonious understanding of each other.

Among the men he thought qualified to lead the races were W. E. B. DuBois, W. H. Fleming, and E. Gardner Murphy.[23] Of course, the first of these named leaders was black, while the latter two were white.

It was no error of omission that Griggs failed to mention Booker T. Washington, the most influential African American of the time. During these early years, Griggs was a disciple of W. E. Burghardt DuBois. His views on the survival of the fittest closely paralleled DuBois' advocacy of the "talented tenth."[24] Also, like DuBois and unlike Washington, young Griggs believed the black man should be educated in the liberal arts and not just taught vocational trades.

Furthermore, the influence of DuBois upon Griggs can be seen in his view of the relationship which politics shared with religion. In his view it was natural for the pulpit to be involved in the political process. In his first novel, *Imperium in Imperio*, one of the leading characters, Bernard Belgrave, decided to run for Congress. The author made it a point to make the reader aware that Bernard's campaign had the support of the black clergy.[25] Likewise, *Wisdom's Call* made a political statement. In fact, the purpose of this work was to refute those who sought to disenfranchise the African American through repeal of the Fifteenth Amendment to the Constitution.

In several of his literary productions, Griggs argued that the disenfranchisement of the black man was largely responsible for the violence that was wreaked upon the race. According to his argument, officials would be more responsive to fairness and justice for the darker hued American if they knew their office-holding were dependent upon the African American vote.

Griggs, ever mindful of human practices becoming part of man's evolutionary nature, felt this was applicable to politics as well. His argument for the Negro's inclusion in the political process was, in the long-term, for the health of whites. He felt that without the Negro's participation to force issues to the forefront, political contests would become mere personality tournaments. Active Negro political participation would serve as a regulator to bring out the best in white candidates. Without it, political genius and constructive statesmanship would become obsolete.

As a young man, Sutton E. Griggs clearly was a complex thinker. He was a man who was well read in many fields. He apparently had many interests in many different areas. As a result, his thinking was influenced by this multitude of interdisciplinary studies. He attempted to weave together into a whole the natural rights of man, evolution, the Bible, and W. E. B. DuBois' doctrines. The result is that Griggs sometimes was contradictory. For example, he believed the equality of man was a self-evident natural endowment. Yet, at the same time, he believed in natural selection and survival of the fittest. Also, it appears paradoxical that he could be an evangelical Christian and yet believe so strongly in inheritance being the determining factor in human behavior.

In the final analysis, we must conclude that Griggs merely was a reflection of the age in which he lived. It was a time when answers were being sought. With the advent of the French Enlightenment a century before his birth, thinking became secularized. Churchmen began to study other texts in addition to scripture. This was a complex age, which produced a complex (and to some controversial) man in Sutton E. Griggs.

It is now appropriate to give attention to the thinking that this colorful preacher espoused after some maturation. Let us now consider the later Griggs in order to fully chart his contemplative journey.

NOTES

[1]Griggs is not unique in this regard. It was the preoccupation with racism and their social struggle that caused Negroes to produce "great preachers but few theologians" according to Benjamin E. Mays, *The Negro's God: As Reflected in His Literature* (Autheneum ed.; New York: Autheneum, 1973), p. 255.

[2]Sutton E. Griggs, *Wisdom's Call* (Nashville: Orion Publishing Co., 1911), p. 53.

[3]*Ibid.*

[4]Sutton E. Griggs, *Unfettered and Dorlan's Plan* (New York: A M S Press, 1971), p. 248.

[5]Sutton E. Griggs, *The One Great Question, A Study of Southern Conditions at Close Range* (Philadelphia: Orion Publishing Co., 1907).

[6]*Ibid.*, p. 51.

[7]Sutton E. Griggs, *Imperium in Imperio* (Miami: Mnemosyne, 1969), p. 218.

[8]Griggs, *Unfettered and Dorlan's Plan*, p. 224.

[9]Griggs, *The One Great Question*, p. 55.

[10]Griggs, *Wisdom's Call*, p. 22.

[11]*Ibid.*, p. 166. A problem with Griggs' explanation however, is that not all southern white youngsters had exposure to Negro women. In fact, it was in East Tennessee where the theory of evolution was challenged in court in the famous Scopes Trial in 1925. There fundamentalism inspired the court case even though there were few blacks in that area. Hence, the religious beliefs in that locale could not be ascribed to the Negro female story-tellers.

[12]Sutton E. Griggs, *The Hindered Hand; or the Reign of the Repressionist* (3rd ed.; New York: A M S Press, 1969), pp. 304-305.

[13]Herbert Spencer advocated a comprehensive system of philosophy based on his view of evolution. He felt all existing fields of knowledge should be integrated within the framework of science.

[14]Griggs, *Unfettered and Dorlan's Plan*, p. 227.

[15]Griggs, *The One Great Question*, p. 29.

[16]Although Griggs may have been unique for his time in the South, he had plenty of like-minded theologians in the North. Such notables as the Reverend James McCosh, President of the College of New Jersey (Princeton), argued that the Bible and evolution were able to reconcile into a wholeness of truth. For a full discussion on the evangelical division over Darwinism see George M. Marsden, *Fundamentalism and American Culture: The Shaping of Twentieth-Century Evangelicalism: 1870-1925* (New York: Oxford University Press, Inc., 1989), pp. 19-21.

[17]Griggs, *Wisdom's Call*, p. 117.

[18]*Ibid.*, p. 65.

[19]*Ibid.*

[20]Sutton E. Griggs, *Beyond the End: Sequel to Wisdom's Call* (Nashville: Orion Publishing Co., 1911), pp. 253-259.

[21]Unlike many contemporary white southerners who used the same concept to justify

their intolerance of diverse races, Griggs used the doctrine to preserve the best in all ethnic groups.

[22]*Ibid.*, p. 243.

[23]Griggs, *The One Great Question*, p. 56. The latter two persons whom Griggs mentioned were only a vague reference. Yet, I am reasonably sure that the E. Gardner Murphy is Edgar Gardner Murphy, who as an Episcopal clergyman helped found the First Episcopal Church for African Americans in Montgomery, Alabama. While in Montgomery in 1900, he was instrumental in a conference that was held where both blacks and whites candidly discussed the race problem and conditions in the South. The meeting's published proceedings attracted wide-spread interest throughout America and Europe. Likewise, I believe W. H. Fleming was William Henry Fleming, a congressman from Georgia, who authored the book, *The Race Problem, and Other Addresses, 1908-09.*

[24]DuBois' "Talented Tenth" was a program whereby he advocated that ten percent of the most talented blacks be given advanced training in preparation for leadership roles.

[25]Griggs, *Imperium in Imperio*, p. 105.

CHAPTER V

The Later Works

Griggs' later publications have a different message from that of his earlier works. Condemnations of southern injustices suffered by blacks were scarce in the minister's later compositions. The later writings are more conciliatory toward the white South. Furthermore, these literary productions contain no efforts in the fictional realm. All the late writings were sociological essays that contained a sprinkling of theology here and there. Thus, an analysis of his works after 1913 clearly reveal a different side to this prolific black author.

As has been discussed, his early writings were primarily defensive. As a young author, Griggs acted as an apologist for his race. His defense was mounted in the face of fierce, racist propaganda. As the youthful defender of his people, Griggs was idealistic. He was filled with the prospects of possibilities. His ideals were the result of theories, not experience. He was absorbed in the doctrines of the French Enlightenment and his era's new learning, which included Charles Darwin's theories.

His publications that appeared after his arrival in Memphis in 1913 had a new emphasis. Most pronounced was his difference in purpose. These later works clearly were not apologetic, but assertive in Griggs' own agenda of social cooperation. They were not reactions to some racial incident or bigoted publication. Rather, these later books sought to lay out a plan for the assimilation of blacks into the American mainstream.

Among the factors that influenced the older Griggs was his lack of faith in the federal government as a liberating tool for oppressed African Americans. The pessimistic, but realistic view of federal governmental aid for the black man, was documented by Griggs in 1925. He wrote:

> Our very vigorous Vice-President, Hon. Charles G. Dawes, of Illinois, has started out to reform the rules of the United States Senate. He may or he may not succeed in his enterprise, but he has made it absolutely plain that the Negro race in the United States has but a poor reliance if it is basing its hopes on what is to be done for it by Congress.[1]

Thus, Griggs counseled the members of his race not to expect a reoccurrence of Congressional Radical Reconstruction, as happened following the Civil War. According to the seasoned thinker, the days of active governmental intervention on behalf of the Negro were passed and gone.

In fact, Griggs took a revisionist approach in looking back at the meaning of the Civil War. According to his interpretation, the war was not fought over slavery. Rather he stated that what was at issue was the unity of American whites. In 1925 Griggs wrote:

> The Anglo-Saxon race has a profound conception that it has a world mission, and that the essential unity of the race must be preserved in order that that

> mission may be fulfilled properly.... The Negroes should therefore bear in
> mind that, in the final analysis, they are to deal with a united Anglo-Saxon
> world. The Civil War is no exception to the rule stated. The primary purpose
> of that war as set forth by the man that directed it, Abraham Lincoln, was to
> maintain Anglo-Saxon solidarity in this country.[2]

An experienced Griggs had concluded that the issue of Anglo Saxon unity was not going to be jeopardized again for the sake of the African American. Therefore, Griggs urged his fellow Negroes to no longer expect the federal government to be their savior from lynchings, disenfranchisement, and discrimination.

Griggs believed that the North would never again dispatch troops to the South for blacks' protection. He cited the Union's refusal to pass a bill, which would have allowed Federal troops to keep the white Massachusetts native, Adelbert Ames, as governor of Mississippi in 1875. While this was not done for what Griggs saw as the interest of the African American, troops were later sent to Hawaii, the Phillipines, Puerto Rico, Haiti, and the Virgin Isles to protect a minority white population's control over a non-white majority.[3] To Griggs this was historical evidence of white unity. At no time did he conceive of this unity being threatened by a willingness to protect Negroes.

Furthermore, Griggs believed that in the 1920s a non-white danger was looming on the horizon. He thought the peril that a growing Japanese military build-up presented to the United States would keep all the states in a strong cohesive bond. Due to the growing need for cooperation from all regions of the nation to stymie the Japanese danger, Griggs was convinced the nation would not risk alienating any section by pursuing potentially divisive issues.[4] Consequently, in the 1920s he felt the black man should not expect the federal government to challenge the inequities of southern white home rule.

As a pragmatic analyzer of his era, Griggs felt it was futile for black Americans to fight battles where they hoped the government would come to their aid. As efforts were exerted by his race to secure legislation favorable for a redress of the African Americans' grievances, such as the Dyer Anti-Lynching Bill. Griggs carefully studied who the participants were. In 1921 he published his findings.

> Today the agitation for the enactment of legislation based upon the doctrine
> of the native equality of all men is led mainly by groups of Negro leaders.
> Not an outstanding leader of the white race in any official position in any
> part of the country has announced an active policy in this direction.[5]

He realistically saw that the agitations for legal recognition of black rights were mostly supported by African Americans. The inference that one may draw from his analysis is blacks should not begin a battle where they expected the white controlled federal government to send in reinforcements. Griggs believed such a maneuver would further alienate blacks from the American mainstream. This would mean a continued polarized isolation for his race.

Griggs continued his analysis by declaring that the days of Reconstruction, when a black politician represented any form of white interest were past. In a realistic vein, Griggs wrote:

> Perhaps the most outspoken critic of the South on the race question that the North has developed in recent years has been the Chicago Tribune. Even this advanced critic is not contending that Negro groups shall be given control of white groups even where calculations based upon numbers would warrant it. It says: "We admit frankly that if political equality had meant the election of Negro mayors, judges and a majority of Negroes in the city council the whites would have not tolerated it."[6]

Griggs was convinced that by the 1920s American white solidarity was the order of the day. Nowhere would whites allow Negroes to act as a wedge to drive them apart. Thus, it was taboo for a Negro politician to try to represent any whites in his constituency. Therefore, Griggs urged his fellow African Americans to no longer expect radical governmental aid. He declared that white unity would not be sacrificed in order to destroy white supremacy.

Here the complexity of the later Griggs is seen. While it is tempting to simply dismiss him in his older years as a mellowing accommodationist, such simple characterizations are erroneous. Just as Booker T. Washington's philosophy contained seeds of black nationalism, so does Griggs' mature thinking. This is most readily apparent in his view of governmental aid for the Negro.

Such views led Griggs at this later point to become an apostle of self-help, so far as his people were concerned. He began to declare that blacks must develop a sense of self reliance and independence. They must not look for some outside benefactor to rescue them from their social, political, and economic problems. Rather, he felt they must act as their own deliverer by closing ranks and giving attention to addressing their communities' pressing needs. He sent out the call for self-help to his race by stating:

> We can decide to try to heal needless breaches in our life as a race which unduly tax our energies with contests with each other. We can devote increased attention to reducing our death rate, to caring for orphans, to providing avenues for expansion for our young people, to the teaching of the habit of saving, to the reduction of our percentage of criminality, to the amassing of property and to matters of education—all of which are social tasks calling for the qualities that make for social efficiency in general.[7]

Here, this black crusader laid out an agenda that the race could act upon itself. To accomplish these crucial goals, African Americans did not need legislation, nor outside aid. Rather, Griggs called for blacks to be their own problem solvers.

Among the men that Griggs admired was the black businessman, John L. Webb of Hot Springs, Arkansas. He considered Webb an excellent role model for his race because his success in business was not the result of extraordinary talents or circumstances. Rather, Griggs said the triumph of Webb "has come as a result of simple, homely virtues in reach of everyone."[8] Thus, just as Webb used common ordinary traits to elevate him-

Figure 5. John L. Webb, Supreme Custodian of
Woodmen of Union

self, Griggs believed his example could be duplicated over and over
again among his people.

Among the characteristics that vaulted Webb to success was self-reliance. Griggs said Webb believed "in doing all that he could for himself."[9]
Likewise, Griggs wished to see the spirit of self-reliance diffused
throughout the race. He firmly believed that there was much blacks
could do for themselves even in the midst of unfavorable and unsympa-
thetic circumstances. If the African American was to rise, he had to rely
upon himself.

The changed tone of Griggs' philosophy certainly was colored by experiential realism. He had lived through the post-Reconstruction era,
only to see the earlier raised hopes and aspirations of blacks eroded. He
had lived through the era that the historian Rayford Logan called *The
Betrayal of the Negro.*[10] Thus, Griggs became cynical and skeptical of
governmental support for blacks. Experience had led him to a belief in
self-help as the way to improvement of the African American.

The metamorphosis in Griggs' philosophy was the result of some new
influences in his life. As an older thinker he began to adopt some ideas
that as a younger black apologist he had found unacceptable. Consequently, the later Griggs' publications drew heavily upon sources that
the earlier works do not mention.

The most notable of these new influences was his acceptance of
Booker T. Washington. In fact, Griggs does more than just accept Washington as an influence. Throughout the late writings, Washington is cited

48

as the authority on strategy for improved race relations, as well as the uplift of black people.

It is clear that Washington's example influenced Griggs' opinion on governmental aid for the African American. In the preface of *Paths of Progress*, Griggs stated:

> The late Booker T. Washington saw with great clearness the new problem before his race, and as he went about his labors he kept this fact ever in view. He was not understood and appreciated by many of his people who did not realize that a new problem was before them, who wanted to continue the losing struggle for further Federal intervention. They wanted him to dig for gold in the halls of Congress rather than in the hearts of his white neighbors.[11]

Griggs indeed became more than an admirer of Booker T. Washington. He ventured to become an apologist for the Washington philosophy of self-help.

As many fellow blacks decried Washington's accommodationist approach to the white South, Griggs attempted to interpret it for his race.

> The late Dr. Booker T. Washington labored in a section where the superior numbers of the colored people would have given them control of the agencies of government if there had been no restrictions on the voting privilege. The removal of those restrictions in advance of a change of sentiment on the part of the neighboring white people would have brought on a physical clash with them. Unless Dr. Washington was prepared for this clash or could rely on national aid he was not in a position to precipitate it. He proceeded to win the favor of the white people by whom he was surrounded and to seek to develop a class of Negroes that would meet the approval of people everywhere, in the hope that they might gain by that process that which the nation was in no mood to give as a result of agitation and at the cost of a policy of armed intervention.[12]

Here, Griggs attempted to get the members of his race to see that Washington's strategy was not an act of betrayal. Rather, it was a measure that worked for the salvation of the African American. According to Griggs, Washington was a realist who used what he had, rather than what he hoped to get from the government, which was not available to blacks in any event. Thus, it seems conclusive that Griggs' lack of faith in governmental aid for the Negro was molded by Booker T. Washington's own efforts at building racial bridges with the white South.

Washington was not the only new influence that the older Griggs accepted. Just as the founder of Tuskegee Institute represented the kind of positive image that African Americans should emulate, Griggs felt that Theodore Roosevelt represented the desirable role model for whites. Although Griggs used anecdotes from the administrations of various presidents, it is evident that he saw Roosevelt as more than an illustration on a certain point. In his book, *Guide to Racial Greatness*, Griggs pointed to Roosevelt as his desirable archetype for the white race.[13] Despite some disappointing acts by Roosevelt,[14] he had shown as president a cooperative spirit toward the Negro. It was this spirit that Griggs hoped to see enacted by men of goodwill from both races.

Just as Griggs accepted new influences in his mature years, he likewise discarded some of his earlier inspirations. Most noticeable among the rejections was that of W. E. B. DuBois. He felt DuBois was hampered by a vindictive attitude toward whites. In 1921, Griggs gave the following appraisal of DuBois:

> Dr. W. E. B. Dubois has chosen as one of his tasks the laying bare of those things which he deems to be wrong in the attitude of the American people toward the Negro. One of his ablest supporters, a Mr. William Lloyd Garrison Villard, a grandson of William Lloyd Garrison, the great abolitionist is of the opinion that the usefulness of Mr. DuBois in his chosen work would be greatly enhanced by the elimination of bitterness. He says of Dr. DuBois in the magazine, The 'Nation', "If a truer Christian spirit than now shines through his writings can guide him — the possibilities of his future usefulness seem great indeed."[15]

The notation of this criticism of Griggs' earlier mentor vividly illustrates a change in perspective for the clergyman. Griggs no longer was preoccupied with fighting back, but rather now he sought interracial cooperation. He now believed that the militant stance of DuBois detracted from the accomplishment of this mission.

Despite this explicit rejection of DuBois, the later Griggs did not completely severe ideological ties to the great Harvard educated scholar. Griggs continued to believe, like DuBois, that the masses would be led out of ignorance by the enlightened few. In 1923, Griggs said, "Whenever in any group a few have seen the light, it is their duty to band themselves together to see that the masses likewise have the light."[16] Indeed, this was a recapitulation of DuBois' "Talented Tenth" doctrine. Thus, while the later Griggs may have disagreed with the methods of DuBois, he did not alienate himself completely from the content of the DuBoisian message.

The intellectual metamorphosis of Griggs can also be seen in his later opposition to some of Thomas Huxley's pronouncements. Particularly, Griggs adopted the belief that change in humans was possible. Furthermore, he believed the Christian religion's message was able to transform those who were helpless into strong, useful individuals. This opinion ran counter to the Darwinian concept of survival of the fittest. In what can be considered his only exclusively, true theological work, Griggs contradicted his earlier mentor, Huxley. In the 1924 publication of *Kingdom Builders' Manual*, Griggs wrote:

> Huxley says: "While people endure the extremity of pain rather than part with life, shame drives the weakest to suicide." Yet, the Bible tells of men so transformed that they were able to rejoice in shame.[17]

He parts company here with the gloomy doctrine of survival of the fittest. The later Griggs not only believed it possible for human weaklings to survive, but to actually be happy in doing so.

Furthermore, as much as Griggs admired and relied upon scientific teachings, he gave greater credence to biblical support for his positions. In his rejection of Huxley, Griggs cited Acts 5:41 to sustain his claim.[18] This is evidence of a more fundamentalist position than had been the case in his earlier writings, which had been almost completely dominated by Darwinian ideas.

The later Griggs likewise moved from his original unquestioning devotion to inheritance as an explanation for human behavior. The older man's thinking on this subject expanded beyond his initial steadfast position on biological determination. In 1925 Griggs said:

> But much that has been thought to be the result of inherent heredity has been found to be only a part of our social inheritance.... No blood heredity could have been strong enough to withstand the all but irresistible pressure of the social inheritance.[19]

Thus, the later Griggs expanded his thinking beyond rigid biological determinism. The more mature writer saw that beyond genetic factors there were social conditioning agents that contributed to human behavior.

Griggs' rejection of inheritance as the sole cause of human behavior was so profound in his later years that he spoke against it in other writings as well. In his widely circulated volume, *Guide to Racial Greatness*, he stated, "It is a false hope to think that the needed virtues may be transmitted from one generation to another through the blood."[20] Consequently, it can be inferred that the later thinker realized that something other than selective breeding could alter human character.

As Griggs rejected the exclusive role of genetic determinism, he began to accept the importance of environmental influences upon human personality. This explanation for life's attitudes had been completely ignored in his writings before 1913. However, in 1921 a decidedly different tone sounded in *Light on Racial Issues*. He said:

> It is held that a child does not inherit the traits of the race to which it belongs, but that the social atmosphere into which it is thrown shapes its character. The most important thing in connection with a race, therefore, is thought to be the social atmosphere, the body of sentiments and thoughts in which it is enveloped. The late Benjamin Kidd says: "it is the matter of its social heredity which creates the ruling people. It is what it lacks in its social heredity that relegates a people to the position of an inferior race." (Benjamin Kidd, *Science of Power*, p. 304).[21]

It is no coincidence that Benjamin Kidd is mentioned in connection with this later transformation in Griggs' thinking. In his later writings repeatedly Kidd is referred to as an authority. It is Kidd who assumed the major role that the earlier writings had accorded to Darwin and his disciples. Thus, the later Griggs is clearly a convert from social biology to the newly developing field of sociology. In this later role, Griggs saw the wisdom in controlling an individual's surroundings. This was especially important for those who sought to modify human behavior. Griggs' belief in a controlled environment can be seen in the following:

> Therefore when a person has a weakness which he desires to conquer by means of a new attitude care should be taken to avoid conditions hostile to the development of the desired attitude. A new attitude needs a new environment. In the matter of cultivating attitudes let careful attention be given to the question of environment.[22]

Consequently, the later Griggs became a proponent for an improved environment. This position was not based totally on an idealistic notion of equality, nor natural law. Rather, the later Griggs saw an accommodating environment as having an utilitarian application in changing individual attitudes and behavior.

The acceptance of environmental influences allowed the older Griggs to appreciate man's ability to change. In his earlier works any modification in human behavior was linked to biological factors. His primeval stance was primarily dependent upon selective breeding as a means to human improvement. However, the older thinker broadened his conceptualization on the causes of behavior. Thus, this caused him to see other means whereby changes in characteristics could take place.

This position made Griggs appear more fundamental than he had previously. In his "mature" years, his thinking brought him into a similar vein to the doctrine of original sin, or at least human deprivation. For example, he recognized that humanity was not born with the mind to think unselfishly. In the 1929 publication, *Cooperative Natures and Social Education*, Griggs employed a question and the answer on the possibility of altering a selfish attitude, "Can the mind without the citizen side be transformed into one that has it. Nature answers most emphatically, 'yes'."[23] Even though his position may have moved closer to that of the fundamentalists, he does not completely discard his old method of reasoning. Readily "Nature" is employed here as the authority on human pliability.

Furthermore, as he sets forth additional evidence, contemporary scholarship was cited to verify his beliefs on human transformation. An example was his quotation of Professor W. E. Hocking:

> Human nature is undoubtedly the most plastic part of the living world, the most adaptable, the most educable. Of all animals, it is man in whom heredity counts for least, and conscious building forces for most.[24]

Griggs' agreement with such a quote demonstrated that he believed education was more effective in changing human beings than was genetic planning. Consequently, he put a heavy burden upon the school. He saw education's role as not just imparting knowledge to its pupils, but actually remaking "human nature."[25]

The mature Griggs thought teachers should devote part of their effort into shaping their students' attitudes. It was through this medium that he thought persons would no longer place their individual interest ahead of that of the group. As an example, he cited the German teachers' method of instructing their students to be patriotic in all disciplines, including such unlikely subjects as mathematics and biology.[26] While Griggs admired the German methodology of instruction, he was not naive enough to accept its purpose.[27] He did not wish for American education to give rise to elitism and a chauvinistic patriotism. Rather, he simply wished that education would teach individuals how to blend into a whole group that would work for the commonweal.

While Griggs continued to base his opinions upon liberal scholarship, he employed the use of scripture as well. In *Kingdom Builders' Manual*, he entitled one chapter, "The Possibility of Transformation." Unlike his earlier publications, which neglected to examine the question of change from a biblical perspective, he did it here. Not only did he contend that scripture supports transformation, but transformation for all men. Thus, Griggs believed change was not only possible for individuals, but groups of humans as well. He said, "If one race can overcome obstacles of a stupendous nature why not another, as all are of one blood."[28] In support of this contention, Griggs employed Acts 17:26 as proof.

Thus, in the older Griggs, not only is the belief in human change employed, but also there is a greater reliance upon the Bible and Christian orthodoxy. While not completely eradicating the use of Natural Law, the later Griggs at least relied as heavily upon the Bible's tenets to sustain his beliefs. In *Cooperative Natures and Social Education*, the appendix uses numerous scriptural citations. These biblical references are used as supports for the various traits that Griggs hoped to see incorporated in humanity. Consequently, the scripture gave his suggestions creditability outside of himself. This indicates that the later thinker saw the Bible very clearly as an authority in and of itself.

In addition to scriptural guidance, Griggs believed history also played a valuable utilitarian function in effecting changes in human behavior. In *Guide to Racial Greatness*, Griggs wrote:

> Civilization is the result of the accumulations of social inheritance, and the future progress of society must depend largely upon this capacity of profiting by the experiences of former generations.[29]

For the later thinker, history aided in effecting a better society. Through the study of the sum total of prior failures and successes the present could be managed profitably.

Repeatedly, throughout his writings, Griggs made references to historical anecdotes. Occasionally, these historical references contained errors or flawed judgments in their application.[30]

Despite the differences mentioned thus far between the early works and the later publications, there is a continuity found in both phases of Griggs' writings. Even though he was labeled an accommodationist in his later years by many of his critics, he never deviated from his willingness to speak up for fair treatment for the Negro. In 1925 he attempted to persuade the white South to pay their black laborers an equitable wage.

> To meet the increased cost of living, wage increases have been obtained for white laborers by means of pressure applied by labor unions. Should Negroes attempt such methods a race feeling would inevitably enter, as the employers are white and the laborers would be colored. When white men strike the contest is between white men, and no race feeling enters. In view of this point, the white business men of the South are requested to voluntarily arrange for the appropriate increase of Negro wages.[31]

Although to many more militant critics, Griggs' appeal may sound half-hearted, it does demonstrate his continued concern for his race's unfair treatment. Through the use of rational thought, Griggs employed persuasion rather than confrontation in hopes of winning some concessions for the African American.

On the lynching of blacks, the later Griggs was as adamant as ever in calling for equal protection. He wrote: "We regard lynching as wrong, needless, and harmful. It is wrong because all men are expected in their daily conduct to obey the law and lynching serves to bring the law into contempt."[32] Here, Griggs' tone is clear and uncompromising even though he is not as inflammatory in his condemnation of the practice as he had been in his younger days. In this later explanation of the evil of lynching, he attempted to show it as abnormal and illegal. Consequently, the older crusader attempted to portray lynching as disruptive to ethics and legal codes. Griggs in his opening sentence nonetheless still established himself as fierce a foe of the practice as he ever was.

Furthermore, Griggs in his later writings showed his concern for his people as he called for their adequate education. On this subject, he stated:

> With reference to interest in Negro education we ask for more than the appropriation of money. We ask for stricter supervision on the part of school authorities. We ask that they take the pains to know personally that those employed in Negro schools are doing their work properly.[33]

The point that Griggs raised here was a particularly grievous problem for black Americans. Poorly trained teachers and administrators handicapped the African American's intellectual development for years in many quarters. Thus, Griggs in calling for a rectification of this circumstance proved to be prophetic.[34]

Not only did Griggs in his later career continue to speak against the American caste system, but he was also concerned about the class system as well. When it came to winning rights for African Americans, he wished a program that would benefit more than an elite group of blacks. As was the case with Booker T. Washington, Griggs sought the elevation of the whole race. On this topic Griggs stated:

> To be able to interest the American people, the Negroes need a program other than that of holding office. This program should deal with fundamental matters, should seek the elevation of the Negro masses and should be such as would result in benefitting the whole American people.[35]

Indeed, none of Griggs' critics could truthfully say that he abandoned his people's concerns in his later years. In fact, he wished to see a broad based improvement of his race. Thus, the later writings are as imbued with compassion and love of his race as are the earlier publications.

Although his later works are not as heavily dependent upon the concept of natural law, we do see its continuance. In setting forth his later philosophy of social efficiency, Griggs wrote, "Let us face the grim fact that it is natural for some things to be divisive and for others to be cooperative."[36] Furthermore, it is clear that the later Griggs continued to believe that natural law played an important role in the social sciences. He stated, "There are natural moral laws, just as there are natural physical ones; and in their observance lies the safety and the progress of humanity."[37] Consequently, Griggs remained steadfast in his belief that human social development had to be consistent with the laws of nature. He also continued to believe that nature's laws were the same for all human beings. In 1916, Griggs wrote "...for there is one set of laws governing all human thought, for all races of mankind, and for all ages."[38] By nature's maintenance of such laws, a message of human equality was implied for everyone throughout eternity.

It was his continued faith in natural law that caused him to flood his later writings with animal allegories. It is from his analysis of animal life that he drew much of his conclusions about human nature. Griggs was especially fascinated with insect behavior, especially that of bees and ants. He thought both had a lesson for human choice, especially as it applied to his philosophy of social efficiency. In 1929 he gave the following narration:

> We cite an incident, reported in the Literary Digest, in connection with which we see the operation of the mind with the citizen side alongside a mind that is totally without that side. A hive of the Apis bee caught on fire. When the female members of the hive saw the fire they flew together instantly, flapped their wings in unison and thus started a current of air which put out the blaze. While the female workers were fighting the blaze, the drones of the hive were wholly unmoved, although they were of the same species as the female workers which were stirred to action. Here we have two distinct types of mind—the type with the citizen side, represented by the female workers, and the type without it, represented by the drones.[39]

According to Griggs, nature presented humanity a picture of life through the Apis bee. Man could either choose to be a cooperative citizen or an unconcerned individual drone. Furthermore, the choice that man exercised would either result in his survival or destruction.

The employment of these allegories were very effective in getting across the importance of human unity. In another allegory, Griggs demonstrated the desirability of eradicating human envy. He stated:

> Among the ants the attitude of jealousy has been suppressed altogether; the queen not being jealous of her royal daughters and often allowing then [sic] to live freely in the home with her.[40]

When human beings can duplicate the queen ant's nature, then intolerance and bigotry will subside. Man will live and let others live.

On the other hand, Griggs also demonstrated through animal allegories the result of divisiveness. He wrote:

> The amoeba, the lowest known form of life, has the divisive tendency to such an extent that it always divides into parts upon maturity, and the parts grow to maturity and divide, on and on. This excess of the divisive spirit has kept the amoeba forever at the bottom of the scale of existence.[41]

Here, Griggs was attempting to show that human development could never be achieved as long as a divisive spirit was exercised. Undoubtedly, he had his race in mind by the employment of this allegory. He was particularly disturbed over the splits and needless duplications among Negro religious bodies, fraternal organizations, and civic groups.[42] For example, Griggs said that the three branches of Negro Methodism have no appreciable difference other than names. So far as dogma and church polity were concerned, the African Methodist Episcopal, African Methodist Episcopal Zion, and Colored (now Christian) Methodist Episcopal Churches were identical. Consequently, the message from the allegory was that as long as the African American continued to allow division to invade his ranks, he would continue to be "at the bottom of the scale of existence."

It is indeed interesting and amazing that Griggs discovered so many moral lessons from the lower animals. However, he was by no means unique in the employment of this instructional medium. In 1909 by his own admission, he stated:

> We are living in a day in which great importance is being attached to what was once regarded as the small, inconsequential things of the universe, a day in which the greatest and wisest among men do not consider it beneath their dignity to take note of what such lowly beings as flies, mosquitoes and rats are doing.[43]

We can determine then that Griggs' thinking was part of a larger trend. He continued to be influenced by new intellectual currents.

Probably, the most recognizable trait that continued from the earlier Griggs to the later was his interdisciplinary studies. As has been mentioned, he was a student of history. Yet, his writings are liberally sprinkled with illustrations drawn from Christianity, astronomy, zoology, botany, social philosophy, and other subjects. This was the mark of continued dedicated scholarship. Though the tone of his writings may have taken on a new aspect in his later years, still the desire for the acquisition and dissemination of knowledge by Griggs was as vibrant as ever.

Thus the older Griggs is actually a synthesis of the Bible student and the secular thinker. Indeed we do see in the mature thinker a more conservative approach to the race problem. This change could have just resulted from the aging process. For we do see change in his philosophy in more areas than one. To simply dismiss him as an accommodationist on the race issue is not to take into consideration the full extent of his metamorphosis. Not only did Griggs change on race, but in his view of theology as well. In this area he opted for a more fundamental stance than he had in his younger years. Coinciding with the theological transformation was also a change on his views of natural science. The mature Griggs called into question some of the theories that previously he viewed as being above reproach.

While we see these changes at the same time there are some retentions of the young philosopher. He continued to seek knowledge from a multitude of sources. Once he gathered it, he attempted to implement his knowledge toward addressing the social evils of his day.

The core of the later writings were centered around his philosophy of social efficiency. We shall now examine it in detail for a better understanding of the meaning of the later works.

NOTES

[1]Sutton E. Griggs, *Paths of Progress; or Cooperation Between the Races, a Series of Addresses, Articles, and Essays* (Memphis: National Public Welfare League, 1925), p. 1. Since the close of Radical Reconstruction the government had not supported issues that would bring fair treatment of the African American. One of the latest demonstrations of the government's lack of commitment to pro-black concerns was the failure of the Dyer Anti-Lynching Bill to become law. The bill had been introduced in the House of Representatives in 1921 by Representative L. C. Dyer of Missouri. This was done in response to the intense lobbying effort of James Weldon Johnson. The Dyer Bill sought "to assure to persons within the jurisdiction of every state the equal protection of the laws, and to punish the crime of lynching." It passed the House 230 to 119. However, in the Senate the proposed legislation encountered a southern filibuster that killed a possible vote on it. Futhermore, the black man's contemporary ally, the Republican Party, showed no interest in pursuing the measure as they voted to abandon it. It was such non-support that prompted Griggs' view.

[2]*Ibid.*, p. 14. The truth of Lincoln's motivations in the Civil War being found elsewhere other than in a desire to end slavery can be seen in a campaign speech given at Cincinnati, Ohio on September 17, 1859. There, Lincoln stated: "I believe we have no power, under the Constitution of the United States; or rather under the form of government under which we live, to interfere with the institution of Slavery, or any other of the institutions of our sister States, be they Free or Slave States. I declared then and I now re-declare, that I have as little inclination to so interfere with the institution of Slavery where it now exists, through the instrumentality of the general Government, or any other instrumentality, as I believe we have no power to do so." Abraham Lincoln, *Speeches and Writings, 1859-1865* (New York: Literary Classics of the United States, 1989), p. 61. Further evidence of Lincoln's lack of enthusiasm for the abolition of slavery can be seen in the fact that it was not until January 1, 1863 that the President issued the Emancipation Proclamation. Then, only the slaves in the Confederacy were freed by Lincoln's action.

[3]Sutton E. Griggs, *Light on Racial Issues* (Memphis: The National Public Welfare League, 1921), p. 23. In addition to the ethnic concerns that Griggs raised there are also economic interests involved in these lands where troops were sent. According to many scholars European and American imperialism were a combination of racial and economic exploitation of non-white people.

[4]Griggs, *Paths of Progress*, p. 10. The official government's position in the early 1920s did not fit Griggs' evaluation of a unified white effort to impede Japanese militarism. For example, when the American brigadier general, Billy Mitchell warned of the Japanese threat and therefore openly criticized America's de-emphasis upon military aviation, he was court-martialed in 1925. He received a five year suspension from the service.

[5]Griggs, *Light on Racial Issues*, p. 7.

[6]*Ibid.*, pp. 10-11.

[7]*Ibid.*, p. 12.

[8]Sutton E. Griggs, *Triumph of the Simple Virtues; or the Life Story of John L. Webb* (Hot Springs, Ark.: Messenger, 1926), p. 54. Webb's life had begun in Alabama where he was mired in poverty, as was the case with so many southern blacks following Reconstruction. However, through hard work, thrift, and sensible habits Webb became one of the South's richest black men by the 1920s. Coinciding with his own personal wealth, as Supreme Custodian of the Woodmen of Union, he molded that black fraternal organization into an economically powerful force for the uplift of African Americans in general by providing jobs, loans, and a sense of pride.

[9]*Ibid.*

[10]Rayford Logan, *The Betrayal of the Negro: from Rutherford B. Hayes to Woodrow Wilson* (London: Collier-MacMillan Ltd., 1965). Originally, this book was entitled *The Negro in American Life and Thought: The Nadir, 1877-1901* when it was published by the author in 1954.

[11]Griggs, *Paths of Progress*. p. 2.

[12]Griggs, *Light on Racial Issues*, p. 22.

[13]Sutton E. Griggs, *Guide to Racial Greatness; or the Science of Collective Efficiency*. (Memphis: National Public Welfare League, 1923), p. 10.

[14]The first notable disappointment that Roosevelt brought the Negro was his failure to consistently credit the Ninth and Tenth Cavalries for their heroic role in the charge up San Juan Hill in the Spanish-American War. Secondly, as a result of the race riot in Brownsville, Texas, in 1906, Roosevelt dishonorably discharged all Negroes in the Twenty-Fifth Regiment without benefit of due process of law.

[15]Griggs, *Light on Racial Issues*, p. 48.

[16]Griggs, *Guide to Racial Greatness*, p. 9.

[17]Sutton E. Griggs, *Kingdom Builder's Manual, Companion Book to Guide to Racial Greatness* (Memphis: National Public Welfare League, 1924), p. 56.

[18]*Ibid*. Acts 5:41 states "And they departed from the presence of the council, rejoicing that they were counted worthy to suffer shame for his name." (King James version)

[19]Griggs, *Paths of Progress*, p. 52.

[20]Griggs, *Guide to Racial Greatness*, p. 204.

[21]Griggs, *Light on Racial Issues*, p. 60.

[22]Sutton E. Griggs, *Cooperative Natures and Social Education, a Philosophy of Civic Life* (Memphis: National Public Welfare League, 1929), p. 73.

[23]*Ibid.*, p. 45.

[24]W. E. Hocking as quoted in *Ibid.*, p. 47.

[25]*Ibid.*, p. 58.

[26]*Ibid.*, p. 70.

[27]*Ibid.*, p. 69.

[28]Griggs, *Kingdom Builder's Manual*, p. 99. Acts 17:26 says, "And hath made of one blood all nations of men for to dwell on all the face of the earth, and hath determined the times before appointed and the bounds of their habitation." (King James version)

[29]Griggs, *Guide to Racial Greatness*, p. 205.

[30]An example is found in *Ibid.*, p. 119-121. There Griggs pointed to Attorney General Harry M. Daugherty as a worthy example of a seconder to President Warren G. Harding. However, history has demonstrated that Daugherty was a poor exhibit for this characteristic. Many historians feel the Attorney General did not back up Harding, but attempted to manipulate the President for his own selfish gain.

[31]Griggs, *Paths of Progress*, p. 47.

[32]*Ibid.*, p. 42.

[33]*Ibid.*, p. 49.

[34]Since Griggs, many have continued to raise this issue. Most notable in the earlier years following Griggs was Carter G. Woodson's, *The Mis-Education of the Negro* (Washington, D.C.: Associated Publishers, 1933). Also during the implementation of Black Studies at many colleges and universities in the 1960s and 70s, a common complaint was the poor preparation of many of the faculty. This was most often the result of the lack of importance attached to such studies by many schools.

[35]Sutton E. Griggs, *The Negro's Next Step* (Memphis: National Public Welfare League, 1923), p. 55.

[36]Griggs, *Guide to Racial Greatness*, p. 39.

[37]*Ibid.*, p. 226.

[38]Sutton E. Griggs, *According to Law, or Life's Demands* (Memphis: National Public Welfare League, 1916), p. 7.

[39]Griggs, *Cooperative Natures and Social Education,* p. 19.

[40]*Ibid.*, p. 37.

[41]*Ibid.*

[42]Sutton E. Griggs, *Meeting the Great Test: Constructive Criticism of the Negro Race* (Memphis: National Public Welfare League, 1922), pp. 14-16.

[43]Sutton E. Griggs, *The Race Question In a New Light* (Nashville: Orion Publishing Co., 1909), p. 7.

CHAPTER VI

Social Efficiency

The dominant theme of Griggs' later works was his philosophy of social efficiency. It is this concept that showed his creativity and depth of thought on a possible solution to the nagging problems of his day. His philosophy actually attempted to address more than the race problem. In fact Griggs set forth his ideas on how individuals could become citizens of their local group, nation, and the international community. This philosophy should have a timeless appeal to all of humanity who are desirous of living harmoniously with others. In some of Griggs' writings, he called his philosophy social efficiency and in other cases, collective efficiency. This interchange of terms is a clue to the definition. It involved the ability of people to become socially collected into a whole. Consequently, group unity is the dominant principle behind this concept.

Unity was so important to Griggs that he did not consider social efficiency to be exercised by a group until all efforts had been exerted to secure it. He stated:

> The science of collective efficiency selects from sociology, history, ethics, religion, chemistry, biology, zoology, entomology, and all other available sources, information contributing to the development of the one thing that concerns it, namely the ability of men to function successfully and enduringly as groups, meeting in adequate fashion the responsibilities that they encounter as groups.[1]

Social efficiency could only take place if individuals desired it. If they did desire it, then they exerted their utmost for the health of group solidarity.

Griggs did not consider a group having social efficiency until it made collective activity its paramount goal. In this regard, Griggs wrote: "When a group has the capacity for concentrating all of its potential and necessary strength behind its joint tasks, and the habit of doing this, it possesses collective efficiency."[2] Thus, for collective efficiency to take place, individuals within a group must no longer think in terms of their own peculiar interest. Rather, the socially efficient person innately thought first of group interest.

While Griggs issued a call for individuals to pledge their loyalty to the group, he did not ask individuals to become so absorbed in a collective movement that it became senseless fanaticism. Griggs explained his position:

> But our call here for the sake of the Negro race is not unto a field of blood. No one is asked to die for his race. But what is asked is that men shall live for their race, that they shall so live that they can and will work together faithfully, successfully, forever, transmitting collective power from one generation to another.[3]

Griggs' elucidation of his position shows he was no advocate of the life sacrificing rituals found in many cultures throughout history.[4] Thus, Griggs' philosophy was not positioned in death, but life in the present world. There is no otherworldly promise or aspiration attached to this philosophy of social efficiency. It was a thoroughly mundane, temporal effort to improve life on this side of the grave.

Even though Griggs believed people should not be trained to make death an end for their group, he did believe they should put group interest ahead of any personal whims. He condemned those who acted solely out of selfish motivations. He felt individualism had to be rejected in every way possible. Especially, he felt that an office holder who selfishly sought to protect his turf was detrimental to the progress of civilization. He expressed displeasure with such a person:

> Elect an individualist to an office, and he grows to regard it as his personal possession. He loses sight of the fact that the office belongs to the people and is only held in trust by him for a stated time. When the favor of the people changes and the office is given to another, the individualist resents what he regards as an effort to relegate him to the rear. He regards his own personal standing as a matter of greater consequence than the welfare of the organization and proceeds to disrupt it in order that he may have a place in which to continue to shine.[5]

For Griggs, selfish leadership was not consistent with democratic principles. He thought leaders should never seek to impose themselves upon their followers. This held true not only for leaders who had been rejected by their constituency, but for those who persisted in office with popular support as well. Griggs was not receptive to leadership that monopolized an office, even if the governed perpetually assented to it. He believed a change of tenure was beneficial to group interest. A change of leadership protected society's agenda from being the exclusive dictates of a long term ruler.

It was out of this context that he admired George Washington and Calvin Coolidge. Neither of these American presidents sought to venture beyond the norm and seek a third term in the oval office.[6] Griggs saw both of these men as examples of personal renunciation. In his view, it was this kind of laying aside of a leader's own welfare that enabled America to become a democracy rather than a monarchy.[7]

Griggs felt that social efficiency allowed for more potent and beneficial thoughts to surface from a society. He believed that a collective mind-state would contribute to a group's progress. Consequently, Griggs advocated that a person should think of himself as a citizen of that community. He believed that where minds were synchronized "a higher type of mentality" would be found.[8]

This collective mind-state was even richer in Griggs' view when it was not limited to the present. When the citizen's mind incorporated a tradition that brought the past and present into harmony, then civilization would be benefited.[9] Thus, Griggs believed the citizen mind had to be cultivated in such a way that it would be transmitted from generation to generation.

While Griggs called for a collective mind-state, it was not predicated upon intolerance. He did not believe that only a circumscribed elite should determine a group's thinking. In fact, it was evident that he felt federated minds would be more productive when the federation was tolerant. For example, Griggs believed that the traditional suppression of the role of women had been detrimental to human progress. In support of his appreciation for female contributions, he said, "Their [women's] achievements since receiving broader recognition give evidence of the great loss sustained by the world by its previous policy of narrowness."[10] Consequently, Griggs believed that the true citizen mind was willing to coalesce with all the various segments within the group. Collective efficiency could only take place as selfish individualism was renounced. This renunciation could not take place so long as some part of the whole was ignored. Thus, in his view, toleration did not contribute to fragmentation, but rather to a consensus. When persons felt reception by the group, they would become a citizen by more readily identifying with the body.

Griggs incorporated Christian teachings as an expedient means through which individualism could be replaced by the citizen's way of thinking. He gave the following appraisal of the practical benefits that accrued from Christian training:

> The type of man that would make a good citizen of heaven would make a good citizen here. So, in preparing men for dying religion has also been preparing them for living. The core of the Christian religion is self-renunciation, and that is likewise the foundation of society.[11]

Griggs saw Christianity as a vital transitional tool for remaking the individual into a citizen. Christianity by nature summoned its followers away from self will. To be a Christian was to pursue the ideals of another, Jesus Christ.

To Griggs this Christian doctrine was more than words to which lip service was given in a Sunday School Class. He believed persons should actually live in conformity with renunciation of individualism. Furthermore, he felt the practical application of such a doctrine would aid members of his race toward the road to progress. In an address delivered before the National Baptist Convention at Los Angeles in 1923, Griggs counselled his fellow African American Baptists in this matter. He urged them to: "Put country first, race next and self last, remembering that 'he that seeketh to save his life shall lose it, but he that loseth his life for my sake shall find it again.' "[12]

While Griggs used a scripture citation here to stake his claim, his list of priorities would not be considered orthodox. Nowhere is God listed in the given prioritizing of allegiances. Indeed, this is noteworthy when it is considered that he was speaking before a Christian body that was well known for its conservative theology.

Although Griggs may have become more fundamental in his thinking in his later years, his philosophy of social efficiency did not become imbued with metaphysical aspirations. Instead, the concept of social efficiency was pragmatic to the core. It was a philosophy that was thoroughly restricted to the present life. As its name implies, it was social, not esoteric or otherworldly by any stretch of the imagination.

Griggs recognized how important the individual was even though he wanted persons to become mentally enmeshed into a collective whole. He saw the individual as the basic unit upon which social groupings were built. If the individuals within a group were defective, then it was inevitable that the group would be devoid of desirable characteristics. Therefore, Griggs felt each individual ought to exert his best, thereby contributing not only to his own betterment, but society at large as well. On this matter, Griggs penned the following:

> Since proper functioning on the part of the individual is the chief sustaining force of society, it is one of the chief joint tasks of society to afford each individual an opportunity to get the best results out of himself.[13]

The social philosopher thought society had a vested interest in each individual who helped to compose it. Consequently, the collective group had a responsibility and an interest to protect individual opportunities for each member's development of his full potential.

Griggs believed that society had a role to play in protecting its weak members. This role was not solely predicated upon altruism. Rather, Griggs saw utilitarian benefits accruing to the society that aided its deficient individuals. Griggs stated:

> It is a joint task of every group to care for its own weak ones. A moral weakling should not be left to become just whatever he or she wills. In some degree, whether great or small, the weakness of every individual affects the welfare of all. This is clearly illustrated by the coming of the world war, which destroyed millions of lives, wrecked more millions of human bodies, wasted billions of dollars, and upset many of the great governments of the world. The match that started this greatest of all conflagrations was lighted by one individual with perverted views of life.[14]

The importance that Griggs attached to the individual brought his views into compliance with many cliches on the subject. For example, such platitudes as "a chain is as strong as its weakest link," and "one rotten apple can ruin the whole lot" were accurate descriptions of the importance that Griggs attached to individuals. In fact, Griggs saw one individual's thoughts and actions as being so potent that he instigated a world war.

Individuals who rose to leadership positions especially played a vital role in society. Just as Griggs saw Kaiser Wilhelm of Germany as the "match" that started World War I, he saw all leaders with the selfish mindstate to be as potentially dangerous. To Griggs the person who led the group was crucial to the group's well-being as well as that of other groups with which contact was made.

Not only could the individual leader adversely affect the group

64

through aggressive action, but also through incompetence as well. Griggs felt that groups who maintained ineffective leaders were woefully handicapped. Whether out of sentiment or lack of attention, if an incompetent leader remained in charge for a long period of time, then the group could not develop to its fullest potential. In fact, Griggs said, "this is the plainest sort of advertisement of the lack of collective efficiency."[15] Thus, group efficiency was dependent upon each individual within it developing a mind-state that would allow him to renounce personal desires in favor of the group's benefit. This was especially true of leadership.

In Griggs' view, those societies which tenaciously clung to their individualistic agendas tended to be backward. Only when individuals cooperated with each other could progress take place. Griggs stated, "the groups in which the cooperative spirit is weak constitute what are termed backward races."[16]

Just as he argued for the merits of social efficiency, he just as vigorously condemned those groups who failed to achieve it. Writing in *Light on Racial Issues,* he repeated:

> Out of the groups in which the cooperative spirit is predominant, we get the great governments of the world. The groups in which the cooperative spirit is weak constitnte [sic] what are termed the backward races.[17]

Such a statement makes it clear that Griggs favored a strong central government. Those who favored states' rights, tribal loyalties, and the like over the national government in his view were not in step with progress or the best interest of the collective society. Yet, it should be noted that while Griggs favored strong central governments, he did not believe they should be elite or estranged from the governed. He was a strong believer in the democratic ideal.

However, his democratic ideal did not entitle those who lacked the group's interest to control it. A prerequisite to rule was the ability to exhibit collective efficiency. He felt that this was the prevailing world view. He gave the following appraisal on the importance of social efficiency as seen by the international community.

> Thus, we have before us the opinion of the world today that a race possessing social efficiency in a high degree has the moral right of rulership over a race not exhibiting the faculty, provided always that individuals shall have all their natural rights as men, with the understanding that these rights are not construed so as to result in giving group-control to those not manifesting a proper degree of social efficiency.[18]

Such a statement is alarming in that it seems to legitimate so many things that the enlightened of the world find obnoxious. Imperialism, and the domination of less developed peoples by a stronger group all seem to be legitimated by Griggs' estimation of his contemporary world's rules. This is a clear reference to "survival of the fittest" with the fit exercising social efficiency.

In analyzing Griggs' appraisal of the rules of his world, one might be tempted to label him as cynical or as overselling his belief in social efficiency. However, a glance at his world will reveal that among the developed countries of the period his view was fairly accurate. It was an imperialistic age, where the strong dominated the weak. This was evident not only among the Germans, but it was the mind state of the Japanese toward their neighbors in the Far East, as well as Great Britain and France toward their colonies in Asia, and Africa. Thus, rather than labelling Griggs as a cynic, we should honestly refer to him as a realist. He recognized the rules by which the world powers of his day conducted international affairs. Therefore, he attempted to prepare his race for improvement by revealing the rules by which progress would have to come.

Speaking to his people out of concern for their welfare, Griggs said:

> So long as the world is not convinced that a group of Negroes has developed social efficiency it will not be in sympathy with any armed attempt to take over duties that demand social efficiency.[19]

Thus, in Griggs' view for the Negro to win any favorable world sentiment, he first had to demonstrate collective unity as a race. Griggs felt this was a top priority for his people. He believed that what other nations thought about the black man was important. The only way he felt that black people would be able to make a favorable impression was to come together in unity. Intraracial cooperation was a necessary prerequisite to interracial cooperation. Other races in Griggs' view would not be favorably disposed toward working with the African American until he proved he could cooperate with his own people. The sincere desire for the accomplishment of this goal was most evident when he said "We have simply got to lift our race in the esteem of the world and we can only do this by the development of social efficiency.[20]

Griggs felt his idea of social efficiency had divine approval. Theologically, he believed his concept was sound and he was not adverse to proclaiming such a stance. Linking the Almighty to social efficiency, Griggs said:

> Does the great God of the universe have the same sort of mind with reference to races? A race of men may be noted for mental ability, kindliness of heart, and martial courage of a high order, but if its internal condition shows that it lacks the capability for teamwork, it will not be summoned to the council table of the great powers of the earth. If this is the law of the universe, fruitless indeed will be the efforts of a race to secure full recognition in any way other than that of developing the capability for cooperation.[21]

Not only the community of the world, but even God judges a race on its ability and willingness to exercise togetherness. Obviously, God's judgment is not spoken of in an eschatological sense. Rather, the judgment will be manifested in the present world. Consequently, it is impossible for social groups to advance without first showing a cooperative desire.

Griggs' theological appeal for social efficiency also employed the use of biblical references. He cited two characters from the Old Testament to dramatize the urgency and direction in which humanity had to turn for a resolution of its social problems. He gave the following contrast:

> The need of the hour is not a Balaam to curse, but an Esther to plead suc-

66

> cessfully the cause of millions, winning for them sympathy and patience, where patience is needed, and cooperation and full justice at all times and everywhere in all the avenues of life.[22]

Thus, Esther's conciliatory role was the preferred way of life. Only in this manner could social cooperation within and outside the race take place. She was willing to sacrifice herself for her people and she also had a working relationship with those who posed a threat to them.

Social efficiency in Griggs' philosophy was not an exercise confined only to the present. Instead, he felt each generation should prepare for its future heirs. Thus, social efficiency required that one live with some forethought of what was being contributed to the age's descendants. Living only for the moment was both foolhardy and selfish. It was one of the worst types of individual behavior. The burden upon the present was presented in the following:

> In view of a man's debt to countless millions-known, unknown, and unborn, it is but right for him to have a keen interest in the general welfare and do good for other countless millions, known, unknown and unborn. If he does not do this he is unfair, is a parasite, is perhaps, an unconscious bandit-taking something from all of the past, the present and the future without giving in return for what he gets.[23]

Griggs laid a responsibility upon the present to be thoughtful of how its actions would affect the future. In his view, man was obligated to contribute and not to stand exclusively in anticipation of being a recipient.

In fact, Griggs said that a scrutiny of world history revealed that the most successful nations were those that planned for the future.[24] As one who wanted to see his race advance, Griggs urged his people to think of posterity. Therefore, he stressed the importance of a careful training for children. This teaching was not only to consist of information for recall, but the cultivation of a wholesome attitude as well. Progressive in so many areas, here Griggs reflected the posture of his age as he laid the brunt of this burden upon the mothers of the race.[25] At this point Griggs merely reflected the male notion that the raising of children was primarily the woman's responsibility. Despite his enlightened views on toleration and social cooperation across racial and national boundaries, he still was a product of his era. Thus, the social efficiency philosopher was conventional in many of his ideas about women and their place in society.

If the black American was to progress, then Griggs felt it was fundamental that social efficiency become an intraracial priority. Within black America there had to be a unified spirit that was so strong that African Americans would sacrifice individual concerns for the group. Selfish thoughts had to be seen as secondary concerns at best. Love of the race should be the African American's chief concern.

Griggs felt that historically within the ranks of the African American, there had been a senseless divisive spirit. Furthermore, he believed that it was advisable that such ill afforded disjunctions be rendered obsolete within the race as soon as possible. In the following lamentation, Griggs pointed to the problem.

> A great handicap to the development of social efficiency is a tendency in the Negro race to divide, and subdivide, to a degree wholly unnecessary, and harmful. This tendency is manifested in almost all of the activites in the life of the race. There are many religious denominations within the race in which the greatest points of difference seem to be their respective names.[26]

To Griggs such schisms was wasted energy that weakened the race. He felt the African American could not afford such divisions within his ethnic group. Differences in name only were not legitimate reasons for black religious bodies' independent existence. In Griggs' view, where there was substantive similarities, but only superficial divisions, then a bonding of groups needed to take place.

Consequently, just as Griggs felt individuals should sacrifice their own peculiar concerns for the good of the group, likewise he felt subgroups within the larger group should sacrifice their autonomy for the benefit of the superior entity. So far as the black American was concerned, Griggs felt such a coalescence of subgroups would enable the race to address many of its problems, as well as win the world's respect.

In addition to his intraracial agenda, Griggs believed social efficiency also called for interracial efforts. He felt blacks and whites had to show a willingness to mutually work together if the country was to reach a desirable status.

Griggs placed much of the burden for interracial efficiency upon his own people. He constantly urged them to reach out to the white race in order to win acceptance in the American system. On this matter, Griggs counseled:

> It cannot be insisted too strongly, therefore, that a great problem before the Negro race is that of growing up in the esteem of the American people, of winning the good will of their neighbors.[27]

Thus, Griggs felt that efforts by the African American to promote interracial cooperation would aid in his admission into the American mainstream.

Griggs made it clear that his own efforts had been directed toward this end. In the preface to *Paths to Progress,* he wrote:

> The author of this volume, for the past few years, has been occupied with the two tasks mentioned. We have sought over and over again to make plain the barriers in the way of Federal activity in the Negro's interest. We have made appeals to the hearts and minds of the white people of the South with the object of stimulating a deeper interest in the welfare of the Negro race. The newspaper articles, the documents and addresses herein published represent efforts in this direction.[28]

Just as his own labors had been directed at winning the interracial cooperation of the white South, he also admonished other members of his ethnic group to do likewise. Furthermore, Griggs felt that now since the federal government could not be expected to come to the aid of the African American, then the black man's strategy had to be persuasion instead of denunciation.[29] Consequently, he appealed to his fellow African Americans to persuade whites to cooperatively work with them. He said to his race, "In all sections of the country, let us meet half-way all who are in any way seeking to make things better for our people."[30]

Griggs was especially receptive to those whites who had demonstrated a willingness on a regional level to cooperate with blacks. He said, "Seeing the need of men working along the line of local adjustment, the Negro race should broaden its mind and open its heart to receive them."[31] Furthermore, he emphasized that such persons "should be treated with the utmost fairness."[32] Thus, it is evident that Griggs felt for interracial cooperation to work, it was dependent upon the Negro. He constantly advised blacks on what they had to do to win the good will of whites. However, very little advice is given to whites on their responsibility to interracial cooperation.

Although Griggs advised blacks on a national level to work everywhere with anyone who was willing, by 1923 he had concluded that the African American's primary success would come on the local level. In *The Negro's Next Step,* he argued that the black man needed to adopt a strategy in race relations that was regionally focused. Undoubtedly, his lack of faith in the federal government caused him to turn away from a national plan. Thus, since the vast majority of blacks were domiciled in the South, Griggs felt it was essential that the African American establish a working relationship with white southerners.

Putting such an assignment upon southern blacks at a time when repression was frequent was bound to stir resentment by many African Americans. Griggs anticipated such a reaction of his proposal. Therefore, to his own people, he advised:

> The time is at hand when those of the Negro race who are trying in an honorable way to perform service as ambassadors of good-will should no longer be condemned for this type of service but should receive the greatest possible degree of co-operation.[33]

Thus, Griggs admonished blacks not to ostracize other blacks, who made overtures toward the white South. Instead, in his view such persons should be given support from the race at large.

The apostle of social efficiency saw a theological basis for his beliefs. He felt that the Christian religion had a vital role to play in resolving the race issue. He said:

> This is not a Negro problem, nor a white man's problem. It is a test of the ability of Christianity to handle that greatest of all human problems, the problem of adjusting race to race upon terms that are fair to both, and that will allow both to unfold all the good that God has wrapped up in their souls.[34]

He saw the problem of aligning the races in cooperation as a moral and spiritual dilemma. Consequently, the strength of Christianity had to be exerted to enable men of different backgrounds to see the wisdom of mutual cooperation. Hence, he believed Christianity was a bridge builder for a divided society.

Griggs believed that his call for interracial cooperation was feasible. He thought that there were positive factors taking place in the South that demonstrated the southern whites could and would work with Negroes for the commonwealth. Citing a common opinion among southern blacks, Griggs stated, "One might say that the poor white man in the South will ever hold the Negro down."[35] However, he reminded his readers that Abraham Lincoln, "The great emancipator," was from this very class.

Furthermore, he found other praises of the white South. He stated that it was southerners, who repealed the infamous "Grandfather Clause."[36] While Griggs might cite this as evidence of a progressive South, he failed to mention that it was the white South, who passed this legislation that grossly overlooked the spirit of the United States Constitution in the first place. Also, it was not white southerners, but the National Association for the Advancement of Colored People who had pushed the case of Guinn vs. United States before the Supreme Court. In 1915 the high court ruled that the Grandfather Clauses in the Maryland and Oklahoma constitutions were incompatible with the Fifteen Amendment and therefore illegal. Thus, on this issue Griggs praised the South for something it did not do.

Repeatedly, he pointed out that Tennessee's vote clinched the constitutional amendment, which gave women the right to vote. He felt this demonstrated a progressive spirit at a time when the southern state could just as easy have been a reactionary force.

Furthermore, Griggs felt that there were some fair and trustworthy politicians holding important offices in the South, for example, he cited Governor Edwin P. Morrow of Kentucky as a valuable official. Griggs felt the Governor's efforts in protecting a black prisoner from a lynch mob was commendable.[37] Likewise, the social philosopher felt Governor Albert H. Roberts of Tennessee was the force responsible for that state not having any lynchings during his tenure in office.[38] Such politicians, Griggs felt gave a basis for new optimism for the southern black. In Griggs' view both Morrow and Roberts represented a new type of southern white who was courageous enough to confront unfairness and injustice.

There were other developments in the South that Griggs interpreted as signs of progress in the area of race relations. He reminded his readers that Negroes in Tennessee had not been disfranchised.[39] In a similar spirit Arkansans rejected a referendum that would have taken away Negro suffrage in "the Land of Opportunity."[40]

While Griggs cited these various examples of southern potential for interracial cooperation, he did not pretend to live in a fool's paradise. He was not oblivious to the problematic realities of the South. He said he did not intend for his citations "to be construed as suggesting even in a remote way that conditions are ideal in the South."[41]

Yet, despite present needs, Griggs saw a glimmer of hope for a better Dixie. He believed that a New South was on the horizon. His basis for hope was the examples given plus others. Griggs said these factors, working in a pioneering way "can lead to a day of astonishing brightness."[42]

Griggs' advocacy for interracial social efficiency did not rest upon amalgamation. Although he wanted social harmony between blacks and whites, it was clear in several of his books that he did not want miscegenation. His whole effort was for racial preservation. This could not happen had there been wholesale race mixing. He stated, "It is the duty of a group to perpetuate and augment itself."[43] This statement was given in conjunction with his opinion that interracial cooperation was not intended to suggest interracial blending. He wanted to preserve the identifiable African presence in America. Therefore, the burden of the race's longevity was placed upon the race itself not merely to survive, but to increase.

Griggs also believed that social efficiency had an international application. He urged his readers to develop a willingness to cooperate with other nations. He especially appealed to his people to exhibit a working concern for and with the continent of their ancestry. This call resembled the philosophy of Pan African-African Americanism. Such a view seeks to establish unity between black Americans and black Africans for mutual advancement. Griggs proved his concern for the motherland when he said, "Let us not confine the acquisition of social efficiency to our own country. The welfare of Liberia should be dear to the hearts of all us."[44] Thus, it was not enough for African Americans to think cooperatively with each other. They must additionally link their struggle for human dignity with the Africans of the homeland.

Ever as much a theologian as a social thinker, Griggs felt Christianity offered an indispensable, peculiar attachment to international cooperation. He stressed the inextricable bond between the international dissemination of the concept of social efficiency with the Christian message. He observed:

> It should be our endeavor to give to all of Africa the gospel, which is the real parent of all social efficiency. But care must be taken to emphasize along with other things those principles in the Christian religion that make for social efficiency.[45]

From this quote, the importance that Griggs attached to his philosophy of social efficiency having a Christian context is determined. To divorce one from the other would be deficient.

Also, from the foregoing quote, it is evident that Griggs had a strong attachment toward all of Africa and not just Liberia, which had been colonized from the United States. This attachment, however, was rooted in what he saw as a woefully inadequate circumstance on the "dark continent." Griggs grieved:

> Africans their sovereignty has departed. In the readjustment following the world's war there was no suggestion from a responsible source that the Negroes of Africa be accorded the privilege of self-determination as was done in the case of many other groups of men. While the inhabitants of other

Table II
Negroes in the United States
(Number of Negroes per 100,000 Whites at each census, by sections, divisions, and states: 1790 to 1930)

SECTION, DIVISION AND STATE	1930	1920[1]	1910[1]	1900	1800	1880	1870	1860
United States	10,923	11,117	12,079	13,223	13,591	15,192	14,528	16,439
The North	3,423	2,371	1,881	1,895	1,796	1,989	1,825	1,769
The South	33,828	37,654	43,066	47,054	51,242	54,406	56,221	55,247
The West	1,114	847	789	781	943	735	701	814
GEOGRAPHIC DIVISIONS:								
New England	1.167	1,081	1,023	1,009	958	1,000	918	794
Middle Atlantic	4,163	2,774	2,213	2,157	1,807	1,839	1,709	1,792
East North Central	3,633	2,458	1,078	1,641	1,502	1,605	1,452	929
West North Central	2,577	2,263	2,110	2,361	2,583	3,401	3,612	5,606
South Atlantic	36,957	44,827	50,951	55,607	58,344	63,106	60,073	66,030
East South Central	36,791	39,031	40,007	49,553	49,233	52,030	49,820	63,001
West South Central	25,076	20,744	30,574	35,507	41,816	48,478	57,403	58,403
Mountain	915	1,003	278	987	1,161	817	515	143
Pacific	1,202	914	734	630	804	685	703	1,008
NEW ENGLAND:								
Maine	138	171	191	191	181	221	257	212
New Hampshire	170	110	131	161	163	108	163	152
Vermont	159	163	453	241	243	319	260	220
Massachusetts	1,249	1,195	1,115	1,154	1,000	1,030	960	780
Rhode Island	1,464	1,080	1,790	2,170	2,158	2,101	2,317	2,310
Connecticut	1,862	1,519	1,381	1,706	1,077	1,801	1,833	1,911
MIDDLE ATLANTIC:								
New York	3,393	1,052	1,497	1,357	1,183	1,295	1,203	1,270
New Jersey	5,451	3,857	3,670	3,854	3,411	3,558	3,502	3,918
Pennsylvania	4,101	3,375	2,507	2,654	2,000	2,036	1,889	1,999
EAST NORTH CENTRAL:								
Ohio	4,385	3,312	2,391	2,387	2,130	2,503	2,420	1,583
Indiana	3,591	2,837	2,283	2,339	2,106	2,023	1,483	851
Illinois	4,527	2,890	1,973	1,797	1,513	1,530	1,145	448
Michigan	3,611	1,660	615	859	731	935	1,015	921
Wisconsin	308	199	125	124	145	206	201	151
WEST NORTH CENTRAL:								
Minnesota	372	372	314	283	254	201	173	153
Iowa	710	798	678	572	562	890	485	159
Missouri	6,550	5,533	5,025	6,475	5,010	7,183	7,365	11,143
North Dakota	56	73	103	92	204	[2]301	[2]720	. . . .
South Dakota	96	134	145	122	165			. . . .
Nebraska	1,010	1,037	652	503	851	530	810	256
Kansas	3,700	3,422	3,232	3,672	3,011	4,5267	4,930	559
SOUTH ATLANTIC:								
Delaware	15,850	15,751	18,221	19,036	10,260	22,000	22,290	23,871
Maryland	20,109	20,291	21,856	21,081	26,039	29,101	28,966	33,170
District of Columbia	37,310	33,017	40,000	45,268	48,852	50,503	49,107	23,500
Virginia	36,724	42,050	45,287	55,300	62,290	71,705	72,019	52,412
West Virginia	7,110	6,270	5,517	4,763	4,476	4,300	4,210	. . . .
North Carolina	41,101	42,797	46,507	40,420	53,153	61,261	57,725	57,300
South Carolina	81,073	105,613	123,070	140,219	149,117	151,519	143,519	141,515
Georgia	58,309	71,422	82,201	87,600	87,781	83,766	85,322	78,725
Florida	41,714	51,611	60,585	77,600	73,875	88,810	95,453	80,518
EAST SOUTH CENTRAL:								
Kentucky	9,401	10,321	12,003	15,283	16,855	10,711	20,225	25,035
Tennessee	22,334	23,954	27,043	31,181	32,221	35,400	31,433	34,234
Alabama	55,553	62,215	73,917	82,630	81,351	90,625	91,201	83,183
Mississippi	101,299	109,531	128,430	141,652	136,287	135,647	116,011	123,596
WEST SOUTH CENTRAL:								
Arkansas	31,800	36,907	39,163	38,833	37,755	35,014	33,738	34,321
Louisiana	59,895	64,009	75,961	89,199	100,143	100,300	100,592	98,018
Oklahoma[3]	8,100	8,210	9,546	8,300	12,523	. . . .	. . . .	. . . .
Texas	10,900	21.014	23,160	25,579	27,900	32,858	44,887	43,400
MOUNTAIN:								
Montana	213	310	509	673	1,167	978	1,000	. . . .
Idaho	153	217	201	190	215	183	505	. . . .
Wyoming	551	731	1,597	1,056	1,554	1,533	2,097	. . . .
Colorado	1,231	1,244	1,468	1,620	1,530	1,274	1,103	134
New Mexico	859	1,899	574	693	1,369	934	190	103
Arizona	4,066	3,944	1,612	1,059	2,435	411	271	. . . .
Utah	223	323	312	247	286	103	137	147
Nevada	634	409	698	378	619	911	916	561
PACIFIC:								
Washington	450	622	546	507	470	484	933	260
Oregon	238	279	223	280	393	299	308	215
California	1,608	1,233	979	747	1,018	784	855	1,264

[1]Figures for white population in 1920 and 1910 are adjusted by deducting the number of Mexicans.
[2]Dakota Territory
[3]Includes Indian Territory in 1900 and 1800.

72

Table II (cont.)
Negroes in the United States
(Number of Negroes per 100,000 Whites at each census, by sections, divisions, and states: 1790 to 1930)

SECTION, DIVISION AND STATE	1850	1840	1830	1820	1810	1800	1790
United States	18,610	20,252	22,110	22,521	23,504	23,268	23,572
The North	2,076	2,345	2,387	2,534	2,978	3,216	3,547
The South	59,857	61,317	60,8968	59,162	57,882	65,907	64,354
The West	898	.....	.....	.....	.....	.....	.....
GEOGRAPHIC DIVISIONS:							
New England	851	1,024	1,100	1,277	1,371	1,536	1,712
Middle Atlantic	2,196	2,716	2,960	3,440	4,261	4,814	5,554
East North Central	1,009	1,014	1,002	950	1,825	1,261	.....
West North Central	11,446	10,358'	22,353	18,867	21,002	.....	.....
South Altantic	68,030	68,014	72,256	67,800	60,253	57,153	.....
East South Central	50,114	47,578	38,101	31,920	25,820	21,190	17,542
West South Central	64,402	90,970	113,815	93,930	123,124	.....	.....
Mountain	99	.....	.....	.....	.....	.....	.....
Pacific	1,116	.....	.....	.....	.....	.....	.....
NEW ENGLAND:							
Maine	233	271	299	312	425	512	500
New Hampshire	164	189	270	323	451	470	558
Vermont	229	251	315	354	345	362	318
Massachusetts	920	1,180	1,168	1,305	1,448	1,549	1,463
Rhode Island	2,651	3,071	3,822	4,533	6,077	5,630	6,755
Connecticut	2,119	2,001	2,787	2,081	2,650	2,567	2,398
MIDDLE ATLANTIC:							
New York	1,610	2,103	2,399	2,952	4,3902	5,616	8,270
New Jersey	5,168	6,177	6,846	7,772	5,210	8,638	8,346
Pennsylvania	2,375	2,859	2,020	2,981	2,060	2,776	2,423
EAST NORTH CENTRAL:							
Ohio	1,293	1,158	1,031	819	630	718	.....
Indiana	1,153	1,056	1,070	971	2,637	5,577	.....
Illinois	813	832	1,537	2,852	6,791	.....	.....
Michigan	851	334	935	1,995	3,118	.....	.....
Wisconsin	208	637	.....	.....	.....	.....	.....
WEST NORTH CENTRAL:							
Minnesota	640	.....	.....	.....	.....	.....	.....
Iowa	174	438	.....	.....	.....	.....	.....
Missouri	15,200	18,467	22,353	18,867	21,002	.....	.....
North Dakota	.....	.....	.....	.....	.....	.....	.....
South Dakota	.....	.....	.....	.....	.....	.....	.....
Nebraska	.....	.....	.....	.....	.....	.....	.....
Kansas	.....	.....	.....	.....	.....	.....	.....
SOUTH ATLANTIC:							
Delaware	28,612	33,310	33,211	31,526	31,273	28,825	27,610
Maryland	39,501	47,710	53,535	55,539	61,851	57,886	53,237
District of Columbia	36,210	42,518	14,520	46,100	19,406	40,000	.....
Virginia	56,880	67,321	74,479	76,550	70,714	71,152	69,009
West Virginia	.....	.....	.....	.....	.....	.....	.....
North Carolina	57,142	55,386	56,074	52,392	47,578	41,649	30,622
South Carolina	143,450	129,423	125,385	111,731	93,601	76,033	77,083
Georgia	73,741	69,586	74,123	79,675	73,507	50,059	56,037
Florida	85,253	94,958	88,901	.....	.....	.....	.....
EAST SOUTH CENTRAL:							
Kentucky	29,024	32,118	32,857	29,780	25,375	22,839	20,519
Tennessee	32,483	29,437	27,281	21,367	21,210	15,140	11,838
Alabama	80,014	76,243	62,562	49,078	.....	.....	.....
Mississippi	105,103	109,774	93,945	78,888	75,261	70,882	.....
WEST SOUTH CENTRAL:							
Arkansas	29,415	26,434	18,375	13,305	.....	.....	.....
Louisiana	102,051	122,402	141,208	107,660	123,121	.....	.....
Oklahoma³	.....	.....	.....	.....	.....	.....	.....
Texas	38,016	.....	.....	.....	.....	.....	.....
MOUNTAIN:							
Montana	.....	.....	.....	.....	.....	.....	.....
Idaho	.....	.....	.....	.....	.....	.....	.....
Wyoming	.....	.....	.....	.....	.....	.....	.....
Colorado	.....	.....	.....	.....	.....	.....	.....
New Mexico	36	.....	.....	.....	.....	.....	.....
Arizona	.....	.....	.....	.....	.....	.....	.....
Utah	441	.....	.....	.....	.....	.....	.....
Nevada	.....	.....	.....	.....	.....	.....	.....
PACIFIC:							
Washington	.....	.....	.....	.....	.....	.....	.....
Oregon	1,582	.....	.....	.....	.....	.....	.....
California	1,050	.....	.....	.....	.....	.....	.....

¹Figures for white population in 1920 and 1910 are adjusted by deducting the number of Mexicans.
²Dakota Territory
³Includes Indian Territory in 1900 and 1800.

73

continents are busy seizing the resources of the land, the native Africans are divided and resentful, yet impotent. They simply lack collective efficiency.[46]

While Griggs exclusively blamed Africans for their colonial status, he overlooked the peculiar history of the continent. He failed to take into account the conspiracy among Europeans to subjugate African lands.[47] Furthermore, this conspiracy was predicated upon division of the continent.

Although Griggs felt that social efficiency had an international application, there is no evidence that he applied his philosophy to its ultimate potential as an antidote to war. It appears that Griggs was so preoccupied with the race problem that he only had "tunnel vision" when it came to the use of his philosophy. He saw it strictly as a way to heal the black/white issue. Otherwise, he did not utilize his ideas in other circumstances. This is indeed surprising, since World War I occurred during the height of his propagation of social efficiency.

There were several factors in Griggs' life that convinced him that social efficiency rather than confrontation was the more effective strategy. Thus, his ideas were not divorced from some measure of practical application. Foremost in influencing him of the effectiveness of this approach was the example of Booker T. Washington in founding Tuskegee Institute.

During the decade of the teens, Griggs found himself cast in a similar role to that of Washington. Among some members of the National Baptist Convention there had been a growing concern over developing and expanding facilities for the theological education of black ministers. There had been some expressed desire for cooperation between the National Baptists and the Southern Baptists since 1900. Therefore, it was felt that the establishment of such a facility would be an ideal joint project. In his role as Educational Secretary of the National Baptist Convention, Sutton Griggs was thrust into the forefront to sell the idea to the Southern Baptist Convention. In this assignment, he spoke before the all white body in St. Louis, Missouri in May 1913. Commenting upon the effectiveness of Griggs' oration, Ruth Marie Powell stated, "He made the pioneer speech that stirred that great body to a new position of thought relative to the ministerial preparation of Negro ministers for the future."[48] The practical proof of Griggs' potency was the unanimous adoption by the Convention to begin exploration of ways and means to take up the task.

There is no doubt that the success of this appeal for mutual cooperation between an all white convention and an all black convention convinced Griggs of the wisdom of social efficiency. From this initial overture toward the white race, Griggs proceeded to become the most vocal advocate of racial accommodation since Booker T. Washington.

Indeed, Griggs saw himself cast in a similar role to that of Washington. Although two Baptist Conventions were the progenitors and supporters of what came to be known as American Baptist Theological Seminary, it was actually Griggs who had stood in the gap and brought it to fruition. It was Griggs who sparked the initial effort to bring the Nashville based school to reality.

Another practicality that led Griggs into the philosophy of social efficiency had to do with the demographics of the African American. Throughout his lifetime the vast majority of blacks lived in the South, as can be seen in Table 2. In addition most southern blacks lived in rural areas. This trend, however, began to be challenged by a northern exodus. Poor harvests, flooding, the South's intolerable racial policies, the lure of northern industrial jobs, and the encouragement of the black press all served as factors in this migration. Particularly, during World War I and thereafter blacks left the South in unprecedented numbers.

Griggs was opposed to the movement away from the rural South to the urban North. He felt that living conditions in the latter was not conducive to the African American's survival. Griggs stated:

> If the Negro population from the rural regions of the South is transferred to the cities of the North, the death rate of the entire Negro population will far exceed its birth rate. For example, it is stated that the Negro death rate in New York City is 70 percent higher than that of whites.[49]

Although Table 3 does not contain statistics for cities, we can determine from the various states that Grigg's assertations have validity. As a percent of the total Negro population in the respective states (compare Table 2) it appears that such industrialized, urbanized states as Illinois, New Jersey, New York, Ohio, and Pennsylvania all seemed inordinately high for the years of 1930 and 1931.

Based upon the association between urbanization and mortality, Griggs saw massive relocations of blacks to northern cities as racial suicide. Therefore, he advised his race to remain in the South and develop a means whereby they could peacefully co-exist with whites. Thus, his advocacy of interracial social efficiency was the pragmatic result of his observations. Griggs understood that northern urban communities were not the utopias that many blacks believed them to be.[50]

When it came to pragmatic considerations, Griggs even offered advice as to how social efficiency could be achieved. The main focus of *The Life Story of John L. Webb, Light on Racial Issues,* and *Cooperative Natures and Social Education* is an explanation as to how social efficiency can be achieved. In order for a cooperative group mentalite to mature, Griggs pointed out that certain character traits had to be stressed. These characteristics were not uncommon and were available to all. He attempted to show this in his biography of Webb. On the other hand, in *Light on Racial Issues,* Griggs listed "The Ten Requirements for Racial Success."[51] Additionally, *Cooperative Natures and Social Education* was written as a companion book to *Guide to Racial Greatness.* While the

Table 3
Deaths of Negroes (exclusive of stillbirths) in the registration area of continental United States: 1931, 1930, and 1920

STATE	1931			1930			1920		
	Total	Male	Female	Total	Male	Female	Total	Male	Female
The registration area is continental U.S.	177,358	93,349	84,009	185,503	97,524	87,979	130,147	65,426	64,721
Alabama	13,306	6,871	6,435	14,407	7,376	7,031	¹2,723	¹1,410	¹1,313
Arizona	208	139	69	206	120	86	(¹)	(¹)	(¹)
Arkansas	5,680	2,983	2,697	6,461	3,344	3,117	(¹)	(¹)	(¹)
California	1,239	681	558	1,157	637	520	779	437	342
Colorado	278	151	127	302	178	124	303	172	131
Connecticut	514	254	260	513	290	223	491	253	238
Delaware	606	304	302	706	391	315	668	337	331
District of Columbia	2,958	1,542	1,416	2,780	1,421	1,359	2,289	1,040	1,249
Florida	7,032	3,915	3,117	7,166	4,031	3,135	5,134	2,748	2,386
Georgia	15,004	8,225	7,769	17,182	8,806	8,376	¹3,383	¹1,519	¹1,769
Idaho	23	14	9	13	9	4	(¹)	(¹)	(¹)
Illinois	6,191	3,453	2,738	5,824	3,210	2,614	3,925	2,057	1,868
Indiana	1,959	1,053	906	2,185	1,150	1,035	1,802	944	858
Iowa	293	158	135	298	170	128	(¹)	(¹)	(¹)
Kansas	1,123	611	512	1,082	538	544	1,189	619	570
Kentucky	4,548	2,498	2,061	4,748	2,573	2,175	4,560	2,262	2,298
Louisiana	11,219	5,838	5,381	12,036	6,313	5,723	10,722	5,258	5,464
Maine	13	10	3	18	12	6	31	19	12
Maryland	5,386	2,803	2,483	5,251	2,808	2,443	5,198	2,585	2,613
Massachusetts	832	449	383	834	432	402	993	495	498
Michigan	2,670	1,482	1,188	2,786	1,571	1,215	1,529	925	604
Minnesota	162	89	73	196	107	89	188	110	78
Mississippi	13,296	6,713	6,583	14,910	7,577	7,333	14,092	6,794	7,298
Missouri	4,643	2,506	2,137	4,604	2,538	2,066	3,761	1,868	1,893
Montana	24	14	10	28	17	11	41	25	16
Nebraska	271	145	126	255	151	104	228	138	90
Nevada	17	9	8	14	8	6	(¹)	(¹)	(¹)
New Hampshire	5	1	4	7	4	3	11	6	5
New Jersey	3,526	1,908	1,618	3,519	1,904	1,615	2,460	¹1,211	1,249
New Mexico	71	45	26	59	34	25	(¹)	2,009	(¹)
New York	7,137	3,790	3,347	6,841	3,634	3,207	3,038	6,018	1,929
North Carolina	12,797	6,343	6,454	13,976	6,928	7,048	12,315	¹2	6,297
North Dakota	4	2	2	5	4	1	¹2	2,254	(¹)
Ohio	5,787	3,304	2,483	5,803	3,267	2,536	4,010	¹85	1,758
Oklahoma	2,106	1,127	979	2,242	1,204	1,038	¹170	16	¹84
Oregon	37	26	11	55	36	19	33	3,343	17
Pennsylvania	7,664	4,195	3,469	7,459	4,057	3,402	6,005	151	2,722
Rhode Island	181	98	83	219	125	94	270	7,095	119
South Carolina	12,368	6,198	6,170	13,160	6,583	6,477	14,338	(¹)	7,242
South Dakota	6	2	4	12	7	5	(¹)	3,971	(¹)
Tennessee	8,013	4,217	3,796	8,744	4,600	4,144	8,169	952	4,198
Texas¹	3,336	1,762	1,573	2,482	1,828	1,654	1,800	21	914
Utah	20	8	12	23	18	5	29	6	8
Vermont	7	3	4	8	3	5	6	(¹)	(¹)
Virginia	11,541	5,939	5,002	11,699	6,074	5,625	12,130	85	6,146
Washington	124	74	50	144	82	62	143	¹25	58
West Virginia	1,871	1,112	759	1,854	1,106	748	¹42	15	¹17
Wisconsin	103	104	59	201	124	77	116	75	41
Wyoming	20	12	8	29	21	8	(¹)	(¹)	(¹)

¹Nonregistration State; data for only those cities with satisfactory registration of deaths.   ²Not in registration area.
³Not a registration State; covers data for 8 cities in 1931 and 1930, and for only 6 cities in 1920.

Negroes in the United States 1920-32 U.S. Bureau of the Census, U.S. Department of Commerce Washington: U.S. Government Printing Office, 1935, 16.

latter explained the theory of social efficiency, the former listed the necessary traits for its implementation.

The traits that Griggs believed were needed were consistent with Christian teachings. Listed in the appendix to *Cooperative Natures and Social Education* are numerous scriptures, which were used as supports for the traits that he wanted to see personified. In fact, Griggs felt that this book was of such pragmatic, theological value that it should be used in Sunday Schools.

Indeed, the qualities that Griggs wanted humanity in general, and African Americans particularly, to adopt were common religious themes. They included: self-reliance, truth, self-control, industry, persistence, thrift, thoroughness, promptness, politeness, cheerfulness, public spirit-edness, and others. Thus, through the teaching and constant reinforcement of these qualities, Griggs thought one would be prepared to interact harmoniously with others. Simply stated, the implementation of his philosophy was aimed at teaching the young how to be a socially acceptable being.[52]

Despite the wide appeal of this aspect of his philosophy, Griggs stirred controversy with other pronouncements. Therefore, it is now appropriate to give attention to the impressions that the colorful preacher conveyed to his contemporaries and posterity. Let us see what others thought of the thinker.

NOTES

[1]Sutton E. Griggs, *Guide to Racial Greatness; or the Science of Collective Efficiency* (Memphis: National Public Welfare League, 1923), p. 1 introduction.

[2]*Ibid.*, p. 3.

[3]Sutton E. Griggs, *Life's Demands,* or *According to Law* (Memphis: National Public Welfare League, 1916), p. 66.

[4]There are numerous examples throughout history where members of a group considered it their duty to die for the collective body. For instance, the Japanese Bushido Code demanded that a defeated samurai (soldier) was dishonored and therefore should disembowel himself with his sword in the ritual of seppuku. In World War II such a fanatical militancy was seen in the Kamikaze raids. Most recently, the world has seen Arabs of the Islamic faith blow up themselves along with their enemies.

[5]Griggs, *Guide to Racial Greatness,* p. 45-46.

[6]Actually Calvin Coolidge was elected president in only one election (1924). His first stint as President was the completion of Warren G. Harding's term. Harding died August 2, 1923 and Vice President Coolidge became President.

[7]Sutton E. Griggs, *Cooperative Natures and Social Education, a Philosophy of Civic Life* (Memphis: National Public Welfare League, 1929), p. 19.

[8]*Ibid.*, p. 41.

[9]*Ibid.*

[10]Griggs, *Guide to Racial Greatness,* p. 144.

[11]Griggs, *Cooperative Natures and Social Education,* p. 85.

[12]Sutton E. Griggs, *Paths of Progress; or Cooperation Between the Races, a series of Addresses, Articles, and Essays* (Memphis: National Public Welfare League, 1925), p. 27.

[13]Griggs, *Guide to Racial Greatness,* p. 7.

[14]*Ibid.*, p. 16.

[15]*Ibid.*

[16]*Ibid.*, p. 42.

[17]Sutton E. Griggs, *Light On Racial Issues* (Memphis: National Public Welfare League, 1921), p. 57.

[18]*Ibid.*, p. 11.

[19]*Ibid.*

[20]*Ibid.*, p. 14. In stressing the importance of world opinion, Griggs proved to be a predictor. Undoubtedly, one of the reasons for the success of the Civil Rights Movement was the role played by international support. This was especially true at that time because of

the Cold War. The Civil Rights abuses in the South gave the Communist block countries an excellent propaganda tool to use against the United States.

[21]Griggs, *Guide to Racial Greatness,* pp. 37-38.

[22]Griggs, *Light On Racial Issues,* p. 37.

[23]Griggs, *Cooperative Natures and Social Education,* pp. 22-23.

[24]Griggs, *Life's Demands,* p. 61.

[25]*Ibid.,* p. 62.

[26]*Ibid.,* p. 90.

[27]*Ibid.,* p. 74.

[28]Griggs, *Paths of Progress,* p. 2.

[29]Griggs, *Light On Racial Issues,* p. 38.

[30]*Ibid.,* p. 19.

[31]Sutton E. Griggs, *The Negro's Next Step* (Memphis: National Public Welfare League, 1923), p. 23.

[32]*Ibid.*

[33]Sutton E. Griggs, *Proper Approach to the Race Question in the South* (Memphis: National Public Welfare League, 1929), p. 8.

[34]Griggs, *Paths to Progress,* p. 18.

[35]Griggs, *Light On Racial Issues,* p. 40.

[36]*Ibid.*

[37]Griggs, *Paths of Progress,* p. 18. According to Griggs, the governor "accepted full responsibility for the shooting into a mob, and the killing of a number of white persons by a military force in a successful effort to protect a Negro prisoner accused of murdering a white girl." Morrow was elected governor of Kentucky in November of 1919 for a four year term.

[38]*Ibid.* Roberts was governor of Tennessee from 1919 to 1921.

[39]*Ibid.* While blacks in Tennessee could vote, Griggs failed to mention they were piloted in their voting by intimidation and machine politics. This condition was so pronounced that white southerners were quoted as saying "Negroes do not vote in Memphis; they are voted." *Saturday Evening Post,* June 10, 1939, p. 48.

[40]*Ibid.*

[41]*Ibid.*

[42]*Ibid.*

[43]Griggs, *Guide to Racial Greatness,* p. 8.

[44]Griggs, *Light On Racial Issues,* p. 14.

[45]*Ibid.,* p. 15.

[46]Sutton E. Griggs, *Meeting the Great Test: Constructive Criticism of the Negro Race* (Memphis: National Public Welfare League, 1922), p. 13.

[47]The Berlin Conference of 1884 was held for the purpose of dividing up Africa among western European countries. This was done to avoid confrontations among the imperialists.

[48]Ruth Marie Powell, *Lights and Shadows: The Story of the American Baptist Theological Seminary 1924-64* (Nashville: By the Author, 1964), p. 15.

[49]Griggs, *Paths of Progress,* p. 11.

[50]Here Griggs appeared to be prophetic in his analysis. Others later wrote in a similar vein of the disappointment northern cities meant for black aspirations. Examples of this literature are Claude Brown's *Manchild in the Promised Land* (New York: The Macmillan Co., 1965) and C. Vann Woodward's *The Strange Career of Jim Crow* (New York: Oxford University Press, 1957).

[51]Griggs, *Light on Racial Issues,* p. 56.

[52]According to Griggs, it was during one's youth that the best time to shape an attitude occurred. Griggs, *Cooperative Natures and Social Education,* p. 50.

CHAPTER VII

Thoughts On The Thinker

The voluminous writings of the social philosopher stirred controversy. In particular, his appeal for interracial cooperation caused many African Americans to view Griggs with a jaundiced eye. As he admonished blacks to indulge the white South, he said nothing to the latter about its toleration of the Negro. Thus, Griggs' appeal for interracial cooperation was one-sided. As a result, he was viewed in his older years by many blacks as being a tool of the white South.

Furthermore, the various examples given by Griggs in attempts to show a basis for progress in the South were unpalatable to many blacks. Many of these proofs were inaccurate and defective in their application. For example, as Griggs urged blacks to cooperate with the white South, he cited the public generosity of white southerners toward Negro education. In 1916 he wrote:

> Throughout the entire South white men in town and city councils, in legislatures, and upon boards of education annually vote hundreds of thousands of dollars more for Negro education than would be thus applied if money derived from the taxing of Negro property only were used for this purpose. It is true that so long as the Negro is industrious he adds to the wealth of the South, and is, in equity, entitled to the education of his children out of it, whether the wealth created by his labor is listed in his name or not, but what we comment upon in this connection is the willingness of Southern white men to take this view of the matter.[1]

This quote served as a two-edged sword. While, he pointed out the legitimate right that southern blacks had in obtaining financing for their children's education, it also left the impression that the southern Caucasian was magnanimous in his concern for Negro education.

It was common knowledge that such was not the case at all. For example, in 1900, Adams County, Mississippi, spent $22.25 for the public education of each white student, while spending only $2.00 for each black pupil.[2] Furthermore, if it had not been for northern philanthropy from the likes of Julius Rosenwald, Anna T. Jeanes, and others, southern black education would have been woefully neglected.

The Rosenwald Fund especially was a boon to the education of southern blacks. Across the South between 1913 and 1932, the Fund helped in building more than 5,000 African American school buildings in fifteen states. These schools were at both the elementary as well as the secondary level. Hence, Rosenwald and other philantropists played an important role in the African American's acquisition of the most rudimentary form of education.

The grossly inequitable spending on Negro education was prevalent

Figure 6. Julius Rosenwald

throughout the former Confederate states. Table 4 shows that from the school year of 1870-71 through 1897-8 that the District of Columbia and the former slave states spent approximately only 25 to 50 percent as much on African American students as was spent on Caucasian pupils.

Table 4
The Education of the Negro School Expenditure of the Sixteen Former Slave States and the District of Columbia (approximately classified by race[1])

Year	Estimated expenditure for each race		Estimated school population for each race		Expenditure per capita of school population	
	White	Colored	White	Colored	White	Colored
1870-71	$ 9,605,158	$ 780,306	3,236,630	1,578,170	$2.97	$0.49
1874-75	11,297,560	1,723,954	3,547,430	1,791,870	3.18	.96
1878-79	10,123,542	2,050,599	3,900,250	2,042,150	2.00	1.00
1882-83	12,730,938	3,632,533	4,306,000	2,221,930	2.96	1.63
1886-87	16,392,616	4,429,323	4,759,100	2,382,570	3.41	1.86
1890-91	21,245,685	5,444,625	5,230,115	2,551,511	4.06	2.13
1894-95	24,432,222	5,011,362	5,670,755	2,761,205	4.30	1.81
1897-98	24,765,544	6,451,935	5,828,980	2,844,570	4.25	2.27
Total[2]	444,709,585	101,800,661	. . . .	. . . .	. . . .	. . . .

[1]Report of Commissioner of Education, 1896-99, vol. 1
[2]Specimen items are here presented at intervals of five years in order to show the progressive character of these provisions. The total is taken from the full table as prepared by the Bureau of Education.

These tables show that the per capita expense of the education of the negro child is, in the Southern States, at present about one-half of that of the white child. In North Carolina the two are nearly even, being $1.17 for the white and $1.03 for the colored, while in Florida the proportion is $5.92 to $2.27. The encouraging suggestion of these figures is that the cost of the education of the colored race has been steadily increasing both absolutely and relatively since 1870. In that year the per capita cost of the education of the white child was $2.07 and of the colored child $0.49, whereas in 1897 the figures were $4.25 to $2.27, respectively. It is but fair to state that part of the disproportion is due to the fact that the schools of the white race represent a higher grade of scholastic attainments and, as is well known, advanced courses are more expensive than the elementary branches.

The States, in so far as it controls education, must, by the very nature and theory of its function, furnish equal accommodations for all of its citizens. The funds are the common property of all the people, and therefore should not be apportioned according to class or race distinction. It is interesting to study the sources of these funds as furnishing light as to their just apportionment between the races.

It is interesting to note that following the years in Table 4, official government publications ceased to print expenditures by race even though it continued to print separate enrollment figures as shown in Table 5. One can only wonder if this change was prompted by embarassment over such inequitable funding as had been the case prior to 1897-98.

Table 5
Common School Enrollment Expenditures
Sixteen Former Slave States and the District of Columbia

Year	Common school enrollment		Expenditures (for both races)	Year	Common school enrollment		Expenditures (for both races)
	White	Colored			White	Colored	
1870-71	. . . .	. . . .	$10,385,464	1890-91	3,570,624	1,329,549	$26,690,310
1871-72	. . . .	. . . .	11,623,238	1891-92	3,607,549	1,354,316	27,691,488
1872-73	. . . .	. . . .	11,176,048	1892-93	3,697,899	1,367,515	28,535,738
1873-74	. . . .	. . . .	11,823,775	1893-94	3,848,541	1,432,198	29,223,546
1874-75	. . . .	. . . .	13,021,514	1894-95	3,846,267	1,423,593	29,443,584
1875-76	. . . .	. . . .	12,033,865	1895-96	3,943,801	1,449,325	31,149,724
1876-77	1,827,139	571,506	11,231,073	1896-97	3,973,992	1,460,084	31,286,883
1877-78	2,034,946	675,150	12,093-091	1897-98	4,145,737	1,540,749	31,247,218
1878-79	2,013,684	685,942	12,174,141	1898-99 . . .	4,144,643	1,509,275	33,110,581
1879-80	2,215,674	784,709	12,678,685	1899-1900. .	4,261,369	1,560,070	34,805,568
1880-81	2,234,877	802,374	13,656,814	1990-1901. .	4,301,954	1,594,308	35,998,667
1881-82	2,249,263	802,982	15,241,740	1901-2	4,386,322	1,575,659	37,887,537
1882-83	2,370,110	817,240	16,363,471	1902-3ª. . . .	4,428,842	1,578,632	39,582,654
1883-84 . . .	2,546,448	1,002,313	17,884,558	1903-4ª. . . .	4,522,744	1,577,385	43,653,647
1884-85	2,676,911	1,030,463	19,253,874	1904-5ª. . . .	4,564,798	1,602,194	46,401,832
1885-86	2,773,145	1,048,659	20,208,113	1905-6ª. . . .	4,608,561	1,617,998	46,140,967
1886-87	2,975,773	1,118,556	20,821,969	1906-7ª. . . .	4,591,031	1,685,723	49,907,262
1887-88 . . .	3,100,606	1,140,405	21,810,158				
1888-89	3,197,830	1,213,092	23,171,878	Total	. . . .	. . . .	914,290,782
1889-90	3,402,420	1,296,959	24,880,107				

ªsubject to correction

Thus, on a subject that was extremely sensitive to the southern black, Griggs made an outlandish observation as far as the African American was concerned. Southern black education continued to be grievously inadequate throughout Griggs' lifetime and even beyond.

In Memphis' neighboring county of Fayette, William Herbert Brewster gave the following description of the fragile educational experience he had there in the early twentieth century. He recalled:

School days were few and far between. We would finish and "Lay by" the crops by the latter part of July or the first of August and school would begin. The length of the school term depended upon how early the cotton opened and the corn was ready to be shucked. The winter terms usually lasted from January to March for the larger children and until April for the smaller children who were too young to be field hands.[3]

Such descriptions were not peculiar to Fayette County, Tennessee.

Brewster's portrayal could have described most of the experiences of the black South during the period.

Thus, with black education being so mournfully neglected, Griggs' comments added an insult to the African American's injury. Unfortunately for Griggs, this was only one of many unwise observations that drove a wedge between himself and his people.

From emancipation through Griggs' lifetime, blacks had consistently voted the Republican ticket. Their loyalty to the party of Lincoln was unwavering. In unconventional form, Griggs urged members of his race to exercise independence in political matters. He counseled the race as a whole not to look upon those mavericks who bolted from the traditional Republican mold as traitors.[4]

Undoubtedly such advocacy projected Griggs as undermining his own philosophy of interracial cooperation. Acceptance of a divisive political stance would make blacks less effective as a political body. Indeed, it was odd that Griggs on one hand would call for racial solidarity and on the other advise members of the ethnic group to be tolerant of those who acted out of political individualism.

Apparently, such a contradiction produced a backlash of suspicion among his people. This adverse reaction was so intense that Griggs felt the need to defend himself on this issue. He declared:

> I may add that never in my life have I received one cent of money in politics. I may add further that my attitude is not determined in any way by financial considerations.... The stand that I have taken is due wholly to my deep concern for the welfare of my people and the good of the country. The moment that the Tennessee situation no longer needs my services I will be free to accept far more lucrative work that is daily being pressed upon me.[5]

At this point it is evident that Griggs felt the need to protect his integrity. His controversial ideas had won him critics whose attacks had now forced the thinker to use the pen for his own defense rather than that of the race.

In his design for uplift of the race, Griggs proceeded from the assumption that white society was the representation of that which was proper and acceptable. Furthermore, he felt that African Americans had to prove themselves to white Americans. From this perspective Griggs wrote:

> It is well then for the Negro race to bear in mind that the white race by the law of its being must pass judgment upon the Negro race at those points which it deems vital in its own life. For example, if the white race has cultivated the virtues of promptness, truthfulness, reliability, thoroughness and persistence to the point where they seem to be a second nature, and if at these very points the Negroes on the whole are lacking, it is apparent that they cannot stand very high in the estimation of the whites, despite other virtues which they may possess. It is therefore urged with all the force at our command that the Negroes in all of their relations with the white people shall take pains to come up fully to the standards of that race.[6]

This observation is clearly an interpretation of white culture as being ideal. Without any questions, Griggs assented to white supremacy. His

earlier ideas on natural equality bears no resemblance to this acquiescence to Negro inferiority.

As unpalatable as the foregoing statement was to the black man, there
still were other controversies to follow.[7] Griggs in an attempt to urge
members of his race to develop desirable habits touched upon a sensitive
subject, so far as the African American was concerned. He stated, "The
leaders of the Negro race should set up as one of their standards the
making of a thoroughly clean and odorless race throughout its entire
ranks, as far as possible.[8] As desirable as this habit is, its mention in public
print was controversial. The statement could easily have been interpreted as catering to a racial sterotype that "Negroes stink". No matter
how noble Griggs' intention may have been, the impressions drawn from
the statement could have been easily misunderstood.

For a man with the scholarly credentials he possessed, Griggs appeared to be gullible on racial history. He readily bought into many contemporary southerners' view of slavery as a boon to the black man.
Griggs remarked:

> Thus slavery served as a sort of shelter beneath which the Negro rested,
> temporarily exempt from some forms of the struggle for existence raging all
> around. Just as the farmer goes into the field with his hoe and helps the corn
> in its battle with the grass until it is far enough advanced to hold its own
> unaided, just so slavery, as a matter of self-protection, saw to it that the Negro
> race had aid in its efforts to live and get a firm footing in the new home of
> the race. But slavery has been abolished the shelter is gone, and the Negroes
> have been summoned to the open field of struggle on their own merits,
> where they must compete and win, or go down in the great battle of life.[9]

For a black man to accept and write such an interpretation of bondage
was heresy of the highest order. It is repulsive enough when white southern historians like Ulrich B. Phillips[10] wrote such views. However, for a
Negro to echo them was ludicrous. The average black man realized no
"firm footing" from the slave experience. Once emancipation came, the
vast majority of freed men received nothing for their years of toil. The
long hoped for forty acres and mule never came. Thus, economically,
and educationally, most ex-slaves got no "firm footing" from bondage.

As ridiculous as Griggs' view of aspects of African American history
was, he was as equally ill informed on African history and culture. Without question, he accepted the contemporary view that Africans were an
infantile people. Again, his writings revealed his unsuspecting acceptance of contemporary pronouncements. Griggs said:

> It is held by some that the Negro race is a younger race than the white race,
> that its spirit is now passing through stages that have been passed by the
> white race. The Negro race is said to be in its vocal period, the period of
> song and noise, whereas the white race is said to have advanced out of the
> vocal stage. In coming in contact with white people, Negroes should bear in
> mind that noise that is not offensive at all to themselves may be thoroughly
> offensive to those older in spirit who are forced to endure it.[11]

Later scholarship has shown that this interpretation of history is totally
erroneous.[12] Without any reservations, Griggs believed the prevalent

myths of his era. Also, again he put the burden of proper conduct upon the black man. Again, it was a clear deference to white superiority.

It is amazing how gullible Griggs was in accepting historical accounts at face value. He readily believed the distorted history of Africa. Without question he was guided by the impression that Africa was a depraved land. In 1923 he naively wrote:

> The marvelous success of the Negro in America has been due in large measure to his capacity for adaptation to changed conditions. Finding himself in the midst of a great civilization the Negro very largely has thrown overboard that which clung to him in his uncivilized state.[13]

Like an innocent child, Griggs accepted the negative portrait of the African continent that had been painted by the anti-black propagandists. He believed the American Negro triumphed "in spite of" his African ancestry.

Griggs' unfavorable view of African history and culture was further revealed elsewhere in his writings. In reference to the Bath House of the Woodmen of Union in Hot Springs, Arkansas, over which John L. Webb was Supreme Custodian, Griggs revealed his ignorance of the homeland of his race. In admiration of the Arkansas building he said:

> As you stand looking at this mammoth structure, before you enter, let your mind roam awhile, crossing the Atlantic and piercing the jungles of Africa. As you think of the thatched huts over there and compare them with what stands before you, you will feel inclined to shout that Ethiopia has at last and suddenly "stretched forth her hand unto God."[14]

Such a view did not take into consideration the Egyptian and Kushite pyramids of antiquity. Nor did he take account of the unique architectural sculpted beauty of the churches of Lalibela in Ethiopia.[15]

From the foregoing pictures, one can see that Griggs was misinformed in his negative projection of Ethiopia. Certainly the Bath House was impressive, but it could not compare with the uniqueness of the Lalibela Churches nor the splendor of the Royal Palace at Gandor.

Furthermore, Griggs' dearth of knowledge of African geography caused him to accept the misrepresentation that Africa is mostly jungle. The truth is, less than one fifth of Africa is forest. Of this woodland, only a small part is tropical rain forest.[16]

Griggs' ideas on nature's role in history also made him controversial. In The Commercial Appeal Griggs wrote an article entitled "Negroes Steadily Recording Progress" in 1924.[17] Particularly controversial was his subsection entitled "Where Colored Has Advantage." There Griggs launched into a discussion of how nature has endowed the Negro with the ability to work in the hot rays of the sun, while southern whites were unable to toil in such circumstances. Griggs wrote:

> The white people of the south, largely of Nordic blood, have shown their agreement with this opinion by yielding the sun jobs to the colored people. This fact is of vast economic importance because it gives to the colored people a vast area free from the intense competition with one of the most vigorous and aggressive types of men. Sheltered by the rays of the sun the colored race could hold its own indefinitely.[18]

Figure 7. Carved stone church: Lalibela, Ethiopia

Figure 8. Royal Palace: Gondar, Ethiopia

Here his devotion to natural conditioning caused him to appear ridiculous, as well as naive. He did not recognize that these "sun jobs" were in reality "Negro jobs"[19] that the average white southerner refused because of their undesirability.

Such contenious positions caused many of Griggs' contemporaries to see him as a controversial figure. Like all such personalities, he attracted both his supporters and critics. The latter voiced their displeasure with

Figure 9. Bath House of the Woodmen of Union, Hot Springs, Ark.

him through both vocal opposition, and written communication. In a brief, obscurely placed, assessment of Griggs' life, the *Chicago Defender* said, "His writings, however, were of such a compromising character that they often brought him much criticism. . . ."[20]

Earlier, in this same paper, a biting criticism of Griggs was voiced by W. Allison Sweeney. The criticism stemmed from a speech given by Griggs at the Central High School of Memphis under the auspices of the city's Chamber of Commerce. Unfortunately, the text of Sweeney's criticism has been lost. However, we do have Griggs' reply to Sweeney. In the rebuttal, the controversial Memphian began by stating he was unperturbed by the criticism. He wrote:

> The article was so far wrong, dealt with a supposed situation that was so far from being as represented that I have not felt in the least degree any intended sting. If I consulted my own inclination I would dismiss the matter altogether, and could pass Mr. Sweeney on the street harboring no more ill-feeling toward him than the sun harbors towards even the blackest of clouds that temporarily hides its face. But we owe some things to the people, and I ask of you sufficient space to explain to your readers how Mr. Sweeney came to make such a tremendous blunder.[21]

Although Griggs stated he was personally prone to dismiss Sweeney's reproof, the evidence suggested otherwise.

Among the charges that Sweeney leveled at Griggs was his silence on the "wrongs done the Negro race in the South."[22] Undoubtedly, Sweeney saw Griggs as one who had an opportunity to be more aggressive in articulating black deprivations than he was. Such a charge stung the minister on a subject which he thought of himself as being a crusader. Griggs felt that his labors for twenty years had done the very thing that Sweeney accused him of not doing.

Griggs wrote a six page reply to the critique, which he included in the appendix to his volume, *Paths of Progress*. Furthermore, in the same work, Griggs found it necessary to include letters of endorsement, statements of support, and even a resolution that was passed by the National Baptist Convention, U.S.A., Inc., that reaffirmed that organization's backing for his labors.

Without a doubt, Griggs was deeply grieved by the Sweeney attack. He clearly felt the need to defend, not only his position, but his personal integrity as well. Thus, as if to give legitimacy to his long years of writing, the aforementioned work also consisted of "Comments in General Concerning the Labors of the Author."[23]

Toward the close of his career there was evidence that the black community had misgivings about Griggs. Many times these uneasy feelings were expressed in a kind and tactful manner. T. O. Fuller, one of Griggs' contemporary ministerial colleages in Memphis gave an appraisal of his friend's metamorphosis. Fuller's account stated:

> His numerous publications had drawn heavily upon his financial resources and the unexpected financial problems served to cool his enthusiasm and sober his thought on racial attitudes. Consequently, he became the champion of interracial good-will and co-operation and the many books written during his life in Memphis were conciliatory and he soon became known as the "Negro Apostle to the White Race." Many of his best friends could not understand his radical change of front, but they still admired him for his apparent earnestness and sincerity of purpose.[24]

As has been discussed earlier in Chapter Three, the subject of Griggs' finances was a sensitive issue with him. Despite his public declarations as to his integrity, Griggs' close friend and fellow laborer, Fuller, three years after the prolific writer's death presented the suggestion that monetary problems helped make a conservative out of the once radical spokesman for the African American.

What one infers from Fuller's comments can be wide ranging and far fetched. If indeed Griggs accepted "hush" money, he bargained for too little. His life would result in shame and financial disaster. This episode was also discussed at length in Chapter Three.

Another of Griggs' contemporaries, who expressed some reservations about him in a magnanimous and diplomatic fashion was the Reverend A. McEwen Williams. Williams came to Memphis in 1929 as Dean of the newly merged Baptist schools of Roger Williams and Howe Institute. When asked about his opinion of Griggs' newspaper article "Negroes Steadily Recording Progress," Williams replied carefully. He stated:

> I would think that Dr. Griggs was quite a philosopher and he not only gave you material that you could read on the line, but if you were wise you could look between the lines and see other things implied.[25]

As was the case with Fuller's quote, Williams' statement was ambiguous in its message. Yet, it is clear that Williams believed Griggs' ideas were worthy of close examination. Perhaps this was necessary because Griggs was paradoxical in his public declarations. Therefore, his associates could not help but be ambiguous in their evaluation of him. Undoubtedly, they found much in him that they admired and much which they questioned.

Other contemporary descriptions of Griggs were less indulgent. At least one black Memphian accused Griggs of repeating the white South's standard response to the lynchings of African Americans. According to this account, Griggs said, "Now suppose some colored man is lynched, you all know that man must have done something, if he hadn't hey [sic] wouldn't lynch him."[26]

In a similar vein, Eldon Roark in Griggs' obituary spoke of the way many black Memphians saw him. Roark wrote that, "Because of his stand and ideas he was often charged with being a white man's nigger."[27] According to the writer, these charges most frequently came from the Beale Street politicians, who Roark said eventually drove Griggs from Memphis.

So far as publications were concerned, such criticism of Griggs was minimal. Articles that were hostile toward Griggs were not accepted for publication by the white daily newspapers.[28] Thus, a dearth of printed opposition did not mean that Griggs was devoid of any criticism among his own people. Although the evidence is sketchy, there is enough to allow one to safely conclude that Griggs was viewed with disdain by many black Memphians in his later years.

Little from scholarly circles has been written on the voluminous author. Most publications that have addressed him have only considered his early stance as a novelist. David Tucker, in a chapter, is the lone source that evaluates the entire life of Griggs.[29] Consequently, the result of scholarly appraisals has been varied and fragmentary for the most part. The treatment of the minister has been only from one or two angles. Thus, the view of scholars who wrote about him depended upon·the aspect of his life that they examined.

The earliest scholarly critique of Griggs' writings was by Sterling Brown in 1937.[30] Brown, who was an Associate Professor of English at Howard University, only analyzed two of Griggs' books, *Unfettered* and *The Hindred Hand*. In this abbreviated consideration, Brown gleaned from Griggs' writings a strong sense of race pride and an appreciation for the attractiveness of dark skin. This interpretation by Brown saw Griggs as an early proponent of black beauty at a time when most of the nation's African American newspapers advertised bleaching creams and hair straighteners.

Six years later, Hugh Gloster also viewed Griggs as an innovative voice in black America. Published in the periodical, *Phylon,* Gloster entitled his article, "Sutton E. Griggs: Novelist of the New Negro."[31] Although, Gloster expanded his study to include five of Griggs' publications, he still only considered the novels. Consequently, he had the unquestioned impression that Griggs was a militant apologist for his race, who refuted the racist indictments of Thomas Dixon, Jr. and Thomas Nelson Page.

In 1958 Robert Bone came up with yet another explanation of Griggs, even though his discussion like those of his predecessors only took the novels into consideration.[32] Bone acknowledged a degree of militancy reflected in Griggs' black nationalist stance in *Imperium in Imperio*. However, Bone contends that nine years after the work's publication in 1899 there was a conciliatory and accommodationist message in *Pointing the Way*. In fact, Bone goes so far as to depict Griggs as a conservative. Bone declared, "In spite of his rhetoric about Negro rights, in the last analysis Sutton Griggs is an old-fashioned Southerner who relies on the 'Quality white folks' to provide a solution to the race problem."[33]

While Bone is correct in detecting a note of the accommodationist in Griggs' early publications, he by far overstated the case. In none of his early or late writings does Griggs look to "quality white folks" to be the primary leaders in solving the race problem. Repeatedly he stressed the fundamental responsibility that the Negro bore in developing a strategy for his own elevation. It is true, however, that Griggs was optimistic that "the better element" of the white South would aid the blacks of goodwill in their efforts. In this sense, we do see shades of interracial cooperation in his early literature, but not enough to say that Griggs ultimately saw the solution coming from whites.

On the other hand, in none of Griggs' writings is there an acquiescence on his part from the race problem in favor of other authorities' solutions. Whether it was fiction or non-fiction, Griggs was always ready with an answer as to how he thought the race issue should be. This was verified by his obituary, which appeared in *The Commercial Appeal*. In that article, tributes were paid to Griggs on his sound ideas for resolving the race issue. Such leading scholars as Albert Bushnell Hart, who was a professor of the history of civilization at Harvard University said of Griggs' approach to the race issue, "He had a deeper insight than the others. He has developed a new view point which is highly important and worthy of serious consideration."[34] In the same article, E. W. Burgess, head of the Sociology Department at the University of Chicago, was quoted in giving his appraisal of Griggs' ideas. He said, "The chief thesis is in my judgment in accordance with the findings of psychology and sociology."[35]

Thus, Bone's characterization of Griggs relying on quality white folk to provide a solution to the race problem is misleading. Despite the criticism hurled at Griggs, no one can truthfully deny that he was a courageous original thinker, who first and foremost thought black people had to be the instigator of better race relations.

However, Bone is correct in cautioning against labelling Griggs and his early contemporary novelists as examples of the "New Negro."[36] This is an extreme portrayal of the author. Although he spoke out against the evils done to the Negro, he still believed in a rational instead of a violent solution to the South's race relations.

The most confused presentation of Griggs appeared in 1969 with the publication of S. P. Fullinwider's *The Mind and Mood of Black America.*[37] Although this author consulted more than Griggs' novels, his study is flawed by errors. For example, he says Griggs quoted J. S. Huxley to support his more "mature contention that social environment is all in the life of man."[38] As has been cited earlier, Griggs quoted Huxley not to show support, but to show his own differing opinion that was predicated upon the Bible's message.[39]

This was only one of many errors that Fullinwider made on Griggs. His entire portrayal of the clergyman as a "marginal man", caught between two cultures is wrong. Griggs was neither freed from myths (as I have shown in his ready acceptance of flawed African and African American history) nor out of touch with the masses. His position as a pastor kept him close to the masses of ordinary black citizens.

Furthermore, Fullinwider forces an unwarranted thesis upon Griggs — that of a mulatoo looking for his niche. Personally, Griggs was not of such a hue, (as shown in the photograph) nor were the heroes and heroines of his stories. As has been discussed in Sterling Brown's view, Griggs definitely was proud of black flesh. Amalgamation in no sense was part of the thinker's ideal design for his race.

Griggs, in his 1909 publication, *The Race Question In a New Light,* spoke of his personal pride in the black identification of the African American. He wrote:

> For our part, we wear with satisfaction, even delight, our badge of racial connection, and would gladly see our progeny wearing the hue of our father and mother unto the end of time. . . . We especially protest against the disappearance of the American Negro as a Negro. Who knows but that he is being evolved as the special guide of the host of the dark millions across the waters? With the loss of color might go the loss of special feeling of kinship. Feeling all this in every fiber of our soul, we cannot view with equanimity the forces at work tending to whiten the race. Hence the sounding of this alarm.[40]

It is obvious from this quote what Griggs' position was on the black man's racial appearance. From all evidence, he remained adamant in this pro-black posture.

It is quite apparent that Fullinwider did not comprehend Griggs. Thus he drew conclusions that were false. He underestimated the minister's intellectual prowess and impact upon his age. True, Griggs was paradoxical and complex in his thinking. Yet, by no means was he a fatalist as Fullinwider says. Griggs knew what he wanted to see accomplished in race relations. He also was wise enough to know that it would not inevitably come from fate. All of his writings attempted to espouse a plan for improved racial harmony.

Reflecting the mood of its epoch was the appraisal of Griggs given by Robert E. Fleming in 1973.[41] Fleming rejected the militant element in

Figure 10. Sutton E. Griggs, Mississippi Valley Collections, Memphis State University

Griggs that both Gloster and Bone cited in their writings. On the basis of only one of Griggs' books, *Imperium in Imperio*, and a definition of militancy that is equated with violence, Fleming says Griggs was not militant even at his early stage of writing. This obviously narrow presentation at best yields a very superficial and biased interpretation.

As previously mentioned, the most thorough treatment of Griggs has come from David Tucker's chapter in his book *Black Pastors & Leaders*. Tucker delves into Griggs' later years and avoids the trap in which the literary critics fell by looking only at Griggs' early stance. Instead, Tucker pursues relevant documents such as the *Memphis Chamber of Commerce's Journal* in evaluating the social philosopher.

However, Tucker relies heavily upon third person appraisals and hearsay evidence rather than Griggs himself. The result is that he presents the minister as a self-serving mercenary, and a failure as a writer. In Tucker's view, it is because of the latter that he became the former. Although Tucker used a very rare work by Griggs, *The Story of My Struggles,* and some candid communications from some of the writer's contemporaries, he fails to chronicle the author's own intellectual sojourn. Consequently, Tucker does not take Griggs as a serious thinker. Instead the social philosopher of efficiency is presented as one who converts from racial militancy to accommodation for economic expediency. Thus, Tucker's view sees Griggs' metamorphosis as the result of external forces. The possibility of the maturation of Griggs' own intellectual growth is not even considered. However, to Tucker's credit, he at least pursued the subject enough to recognize the change in Griggs. This alone sets his work apart from his predecessors.

In the final analysis, we can see that there is a wide variation in opinions about Griggs. Some of his contemporaries saw him as beginning as a radical and becoming an "Uncle Tom" by the end of his life. Others were ambivalent about him. Still, there were many who continued to have faith in his labors for the elevation of African Americans.

The reason for this vast array of opinions is research on Griggs has not been thorough nor complete. At best there have been attempts at simplifying a very complex social thinker who infused both Christian teachings and science in his ideas. Consequently, segmentation and partial investigations have resulted in only variegated confusion as to who Griggs was and what he meant to his era.

Therefore, let us now turn our attention to an analytical interpretation of the total life contributions of this prolific writer, energetic orator, and concerned social thinker. We shall attempt to appraise his work and define his proper place in history.

NOTES

[1]Sutton E. Griggs, *Life's Demands, or According to Law* (Memphis: National Public Welfare League, 1916), p. 76.

[2]John Hope Franklin and Alfred A. Moss, Jr., *From Slavery to Freedom: A History of Negro Americans* (6th ed.; New York: Alfred A. Knopf, 1988), p. 243.

[3]William Herbert Brewster, *Tribute: The Life of Dr. William Herbert Brewster* (Memphis: The Brewster House of Sermon Songs, Christian Literature and Dramatic Arts, 1982), p. 17.

[4]Sutton E. Griggs, *The Negro's Next Step* (Memphis: National Public Welfare League, 1923), p. 50.

[5]Sutton E. Griggs, *Paths of Progress; or Co-operation Between the Races, a Series of Addresses, Articles, and Essays* (Memphis: National Public Welfare League, 1925), p. 24.

[6]Griggs, *Life's Demands*, pp. 79-80.

[7]Unfortunately, most of Griggs' critics were oral. It must be remembered that this was a period when few blacks were published. Thus, we are totally dependent upon secondary sources for any contemporary criticism of him. The two primary sources that probably would have yielded some critical assessments of Griggs, *The Chicago Defender* and *The Memphis World*, two black newspapers, have no surviving copies of much of the decade of the 1920's. This was the period when the bulk of Griggs' controversial writings were published. The only sources still surviving that speak of criticism of him are his own reactions to them and comments noted by third parties.

[8]*Ibid.*, p. 83.

[9]*Ibid.*, p. 128.

[10]The kind of mythical apology that Phillips gave for southern slavery can be seen in the following quote from Ulrich B. Phillips' *American Negro Slavery: A Survey of the Supply, Employment and Control of Negro Labor as Determined by the Plantation Regime* (2nd paperback ed.; Baton Rouge: Louisiana State Univeristy Press, 1969), pp. 327-328. Phillips said, "The general regime was in fact shaped by mutual requirements, concessions and understandings, producing reciprocal codes of conventional morality. Masters of the standard type promoted Christianity and the customs of marriage and parental care, and they instructed as much by example as by precept; they gave occasional holidays, rewards and indulgences, and permitted as large a degree of liberty as they thought the slaves could be trusted not to abuse; they refrained from selling slaves except under the stress of circumstances; they voided cruel, vindictive and captious punishments, and endeavored to inspire effort through affection rather than through fear; and they were content with achieving quite moderate industrial results. In short their despotism, so far as it might properly be so called, was benevolent in intent and on the whole beneficial in effect."

[11]Griggs, *Life's Demands*, p. 85.

[12]Most modern scholars believe the earliest humans were dark skinned and located in the sub-Saharan region of Africa. For a fuller discussion of this see "The Search for Adam and Eve" *Newsweek*, CX1 (January 11, 1988), pp. 46-52 and Anthony Esler, *The Human Venture: The Great Enterprise, A World History to 1500* (Englewood Cliffs, N.J.: Prentice-Hall, Inc., 1986), p. 103.

[13]Griggs, *The Negro's Next Step*, p. 45. As has been discussed in Chapter Two, W. E. B. DuBois and Carter G. Woodson, two contemporaries of Griggs did not share his negative assumptions of the African Negro as an infantile people. Furthermore, within a decade of Griggs' death such African American historians as Lorenzo Green and J. A. Rogers were presenting a picture of Africa that showed some remarkable advancements in transportation, metallurgy, and other areas which were far in advance of European efforts in the same fields during the medieval epoch.

[14]Sutton E. Griggs, *Triumph of the Simple Virtues; or the Life Story of John L. Webb* (Hot Springs, Ark.: Messenger, 1926), p. 23.

[15]These churches were built during the reign of Lalibela (c. 1181-c.1221). However, they were not Ethiopia's first venture in great buildings. Robert W. July's *A History of the African People* (New York: Charles Scribner's Sons, 1970), p. 91 records that these churches "followed in the long tradition of religious architecture already widely practiced in Ethiopia and utilized ancient motifs such as the shaped arches inspired by the summit of the great stele at Axum."

[16]Esler, *The Human Venture,* p. 103.

[17]Sutton E. Griggs, *The Commercial Appeal,* February 28, 1924, p. 24.

[18]*Ibid.* During this period, the NAACP and its followers would have most assuredly objected to this professed biological racial difference. It was during this same period that the Civil Rights organization was pressing for equality in voting, and an end to segregation and discrimination. Griggs' pronouncements would have questioned the wisdom of such a platform. Social and political equality would seem impossible if his genetic assumptions were believed.

[19]Griggs thought these "sun jobs" were proof that blacks were better off in the South than in the North. He stated in the North the Negro did not have the intense rays of the sun to protect his employment. However, the truth of the matter was the North had its "Negro jobs" as well. These jobs were most often hot, dirty, and dangerous. For a description at length of "Negro jobs" see Abdul Alkalimat and Associates, *Introduction to Afro-American Studies: A Peoples College Primer* (Chicago: Twenty-first Century Books and Publications, 1986), pp. 108-109.

[20]*Chicago Defender,* January 7, 1933, p. 13.

[21]Griggs, *Paths to Progress,* p. 105. As has been pointed out above, the text of Sweeney's comments are lost. An extensive investigation that led to the *Chicago Defender,* the Illinois State Historical Society, the University of Chicago, and the University of Illinois all proved futile in attempting to find copies of the 1923-1925 *Chicago Defender.* Thus, we are totally dependent upon Griggs' rebuttal as a secondary source.

[22]*Ibid.*

[23]*Ibid.,* pp. 115-117.

[24]T. O. Fuller, *History of the Negro Baptists of Tennessee* (Memphis: by Author, 1936), pp. 76-77.

[25]Interview conducted by Randolph Meade Walker, with Rev. A. McEwen Williams, Pastor, St. John Baptist Church, Memphis, Tennessee, October 15, 1975.

[26]Fred.L. Hutchins to David Tucker, March 19, 1969 as quoted in David M. Tucker, *Black Pastors and Leaders: Memphis, 1819-1972* (Memphis: Memphis State University Press, 1975), p. 81.

[27]Eldon F. Roark, Jr. *Memphis Press Scimitar,* January 4, 1933, p. 7.

[28]Tucker, *Black Pastors and Leaders,* p. 81.

[29]*Ibid.,* pp. 71-86.

[30]Sterling Brown, *The Negro in American Fiction* (Washington, D.C.: The Associates in Negro Folk Education, 1937), pp. 100-101.

[31]Hugh M. Gloster, "Sutton E. Griggs: Novelist of the New Negro," Phylon, IV (Fourth Quarter, 1943), pp. 335-345.

[32]Robert A. Bone, *The Negro Novel in America* (Revised ed.; New Haven: Yale University Press, Inc., 1965), pp. 32-35.

[33]*Ibid.,* p. 34.

[34]Roark, *Memphis Press Scimitar,* p. 7.

[35]*Ibid.*

[36]This term was coined by Alain Locke in the 1920's. It was descriptive of the mood of assertion that World War I helped to inspire in black manhood.

[37]S. P. Fullinwider, *The Mind and Mood of Black America* (Homewood, Illinois: The Dorsey Press, 1969), pp. 73-77.

[38]*Ibid.,* p. 74. While Fullinwider says that Griggs here is referring to J. S. Huxley, Griggs' publication simply says Huxley. A shortcoming of Griggs' writing was he oftimes only employed last names. My own personal opinion is here Griggs was not speaking of J. S., but his grandfather, Thomas, who he referred to elsewhere by the first and last name.

[39]Sutton E. Griggs, *Kingdom Builder's Manual, Companion Book to Guide to Racial Greatness* (Memphis: National Public Welfare League, 1924), p. 56.

[40]Sutton E. Griggs, *The Race Question In A New Light* (Nashville: Orion Publishing Co., 1909), pp. 46-47.

[41]Robert E. Fleming, "Sutton E. Griggs: Militant Black Novelist," *Phylon, XXXIV,* March, 1973), pp. 73-77.

CHAPTER VIII

Appraisal

As has been noted, the studies on Sutton E. Griggs thus far are inadequate. It is most evident that those who have only considered his fictional writings have a partial view of his career as an author and thinker. On the other hand, to simply dismiss him as a money hungry Uncle Tom for his later views is to have no appreciation for the times in which he lived, nor the depth of Griggs' intellectual sojourn. Thus, to give a comprehensive characterization of him as a philosopher, one must not look for superficial explanations. Both the man and his time were complex and contradictory.

Indeed, to understand the metamorphosis that took place in Griggs' thinking, we must thoroughly comprehend the culture in which this clergyman lived. From birth until death, Griggs was domiciled in the South. Not only were Jim Crow laws strictly enforced during his day, but, the threat of physical harassment of African Americans throughout the region was a constant part of each day's activities. Black people lived under the shadow of racial violence.

The terrorist activities of mobs were so ingrained within the late nineteenth and early twentieth centuries' culture that they were given semi-legal status. In 1898, the president of the National Baptist Convention reported, "There seems to be an unholy alliance between some of the officers of the law and the mob to overturn the very foundation on which our government rests."[1] This dismal picture did not change so far as blacks were concerned within Griggs' lifetime. Evidence of the "unholy alliance" between racist vigilantes and the legal process was blatantly displayed in a 1925 headline in *The Commercial Appeal*. It reported that two hundred members of the Pine Bluff, Arkansas, Ku Klux Klan "were to join forces with a posse of several hundred Cleveland County men."[2] The posse was searching for two Negro men who were suspected of murder in Arkansas. The newspaper's routine reporting of such an outrageous alliance between a known terrorist organization and the law showed how little value black life had in Griggs' lifetime.

An integral part of the era's lynching was the fiendish desire for a victim's body parts as memorabilia. James Weldon Johnson gave the following description from the "Memphis Press" of the lynching of Ell Person, which occurred on Macon Road just outside the Memphis city limits in 1918:

> After Ell Person, the ax fiend had been burned to death, many members of the crowd helped to mutilate the body. One man, his hands covered with blood, cut out the heart and the lungs and offered them as souvenirs to the

crowd. Others cut off toes and pieces of clothing, and finally the head was
severed from the body and placed on the bank leading to the road, so all
might see. The head and a leg were later brought to Memphis.[3]

Such a vivid description showed that the killing of blacks was almost on
the same level as the killing of a hog. It was a festival, a public spectacle
for those who relished such dastardly deeds.

Table 1 (Chapter I) demonstrated that during all but the first ten years
of Griggs' life, the government had statistics to prove that not a year
passed in which a Negro was exempt from the cruel and sordid practice
of lynching. Thus, he knew the horrors of mob violence throughout his
lifetime.

Although lynchings usually resulted from the accusation that a black
male had assaulted a white female, it was not always the case. Sometimes
black people were physically intimidated without any cause or suspicion
whatsoever. For example in 1919 *The Commercial Appeal* reported:

While he was seated on the curb at Main Street and Union Avenue yesterday
evening at 6:30 o'clock, Toney Reinhart, 21, negro, Turley Street, was attacked by four white men, three of whom, according to the police, were
intoxicated. Reinhart was waiting for his uncle, to inform the latter that his
sister had died in St. Louis. One of the assailants asked Reinhart if he wished
to make 25 cents. "I told him I had to stay on the corner. Then he asked me
if I had any ancestors," Reinhart related, "I told him no." Not knowing the
meaning of the word 'ancestors,' Reinhart was somewhat puzzled at the
question and stood up to edge away from the quartet. The white men followed. One drew an automatic pistol, while another caught his trousers and
tore the left leg completely off, it is alleged, and the other two threw him to
the ground and loosened several teeth and gave Reinhart a severe beating
about the head and body.[4]

This narration demonstrates how the African American during the period lived under a constant threat to his person. He did not need to be a
suspect, but just be in the wrong place at the wrong time and he would
be manhandled.

While most of the violence was associated with the South, where the
majority of African Americans lived, other areas of the country were not
exempt. For example, it was the race riot of 1908 in Springfield, Illinois,
that spurred concerned persons of both races to meet in New York in
1909 to found the National Association for the Advancement of Colored
People. In 1925, a mob tried to lynch a black man who was accused of
having attacked a four year old white girl in Indiana Harbor, near Chicago.[5] Also, it was reported that in Chicago in the same year there were
"at least 25,000 drug addicts and morons," who roamed the streets of
the Metropolis threatening white women and children.[6] In response, this
northern city gave orders to its police "to round them up and hold them
under arrest."[7]

Thus, it did not matter whether the black man was in the South or the
North, he was presumed guilty until he could prove otherwise. In both
regions he was viewed in unfavorable terms. His presence was not desired any more in the North than it was in the South. This was exemplified

by the restricted housing that gave rise to northern urban slums, which resulted in overcrowding, crime, and deprivation. As has been demonstrated in Table 3 (Chapter VI) an inordinately high death rate among African Americans in northern cities resulted.

Yet, the black man still had an allegiance for whatever locale was his home. For example, the 1908 description that G. P. Hamilton gave of Memphis was so favorable that one would wonder how could the atrocities already described take place anywhere near the metropolis. For example, Hamilton gave the following appraisal of race relations in the Bluff City:

> The relationship between the two races in Memphis is as friendly and cordial as can be reasonably expected. Occasionally, there may be rash and intemperate men of both races who, if not restrained by conservative element, would possibly try to jeopardize this friendly relationship and cause unnecessary friction and strife; but the great majority of both races are sincerely desirous of peace.[8]

Such favorable impressions of the city were given by other black Memphians' as well. For example, when it came to political expression, Blair Hunt thought blacks in Memphis were better off than those in surrounding communities. As proof, he offered the fact that his grandfather had served as an alderman and his uncle as county registrar.[9]

When asked if Memphis was a better place for blacks to live than most other areas, A. McEwen Williams responded in a more candid and philosophical manner.

> I don't know that it was actually so. In every community, we felt that our town was the best. When I lived in Nashville, we said it was the best place. When I came to Memphis, we said this is the best place. In Chattanooga, we said that was the best place. So, each little community had its own view; its prejudice lies in the city there.[10]

Williams had lived enough places to recognize this tendency in residences. In 1921 he had been a pastor in Toronto, Canada. In the late twenties, he returned to his native Nashville to work at his Alma Mater, Roger Williams University. After it merged in 1929 with Howe Institute in Memphis, he moved to the West Tennessee city. Consequently, he had sufficient experience to witness how the members of each community became attached to it. Thus, an outsider might find displeasure in it, but the residents thought of it as the best place to live.

Since Sutton E. Griggs had spent all his life as an occupant of the South, one can understand his opposition to the northern migration of blacks. If it was indeed regional prejudices that prompted Griggs' desire for continued black residency in the South, he was not alone as shown in the positions of Hamilton and Hunt.

While it was true the South had its share of violence and intimidation of blacks, it still was home to the vast majority of the race. Consequently, there were many who were not willing to readily renounce their southern roots, no matter how unappealing it looked to observers. Indeed, it appeared Sutton Griggs was of such an opinion.

Figure 11. Hambone's
Meditations

Yet, the South's racial problems persisted. The oppression of southern blacks was not limited to physical abuse. There were numerous psychological forces of intimidation that served as constant messages of ridicule of the African American. A favorite device was the public portrayal of the African American as a stupid, docile figure. Appearing daily in *The Commercial Appeal* in Memphis during Griggs' residency (1913-1930) was "Hambone's Meditations." Through the use of broken English and irrational thought, the darkened cartoon character, Hambone, depicted black people as childlike and thoughtless. The foregoing cartoon is such an example. Such parodies of black life not only reinforced white racism, but also made the African American have negative thoughts about himself.

"Hambone's Meditations" were also used to editorialize. This was especially true of issues that were of great importance to the African American. For example, the following cartoon was used to show the futility in the northern black migration. This cartoon used a darkened character to speak white sentiments. The effect of such a device was division and dissention among black people. Some accepted the Hambone message as that of the African American. Thus, such persons became an echo of white concerns rather than independent thinkers who considered their people's best interests.

During Griggs' lifetime the subhuman status of the African American was routinely reinforced. Seemingly innocent devices carried a potent, poisonous messsage of ridicule of black life. Toys, decorations, and household items all used black images in a vile and derogatory manner. In 1923 *The Commercial Appeal* carried an advertisement for the Ala-

102

Figure 12. Hambone's
Meditations

bama Coon Jigger. The mere name of this toy carried a double insult to black people. The South had long used the term "Coon" as a derisive term for the Negro. Furthermore, the assonance of Jigger with "Nigger" carried an implied contemptuous message.

Such was the trend throughout the South during Griggs' lifetime. Daily newspapers were quick to carry stories that showed the black man as a murderer, robber, or other undesirable deviant. Seldom did favorable coverage of African Americans appear in print. Usually when it did, it was done as an example of what white society thought was a desirable Negro.

This was the case when Robert R. Moton, the principal of Tuskegee Institute, went to France following the cessation of hostilities in World War I. Moton attempted to prepare the African American soldier for his return to the United States by stating the black veteran must not continue to look for the freedoms in America that he experienced abroad. *The Commercial Appeal* gave a ready endorsement to such advice in an article entitled "Friend of His Race."[11] The paper stated, "The negroes will do well to follow the advice of Principal Moton."[12]

Such patronizing arrogance was not uncommon in Griggs' era. Whites took for granted they knew what was best for African Americans. Thus, they were not hesitant to reveal their prejudiced opinions.

On the other hand, it was extremely rare that blacks were able to freely express themselves in a widely disseminated publication. Southern daily newspapers only carried stories by or about African Americans that were

Figure 13. Alabama Coon Jigger

consistent with the status quo of the white controlled region. Likewise, book publishers were reluctant to print black literature. Prior to the Harlem Renaissance, black writers particularly found it difficult to be accepted by a major publisher. Only a handful of writers were printed by white owned establishments at this early date. Even the best known of the scholarly authors, W. E. B. DuBois, was unable to get some of his manuscripts circulated.[13]

If it was difficult for such a well known national figure like DuBois to be published, it is certainly understandable why Griggs had all of his writings go to a private press. Furthermore, toward the end of his life, the Great Depression made a difficult situation even more distressing. As the twenties came to a close, black writers saw their prospects diminish as the country's economic woes undermined the Harlem Renaissance's gains.

One of the few black writers who thrived in the immediate post Griggs' years was Zora Neale Hurston.[14] However, her success was predicated upon a compromising stance. Her early career overlapped Griggs' later writings in terms of a conciliatory tone.[15] Her success and overtures to white America combined to show that blacks either had to say what white America wanted or not be published.

Although Griggs was never printed in his lifetime by a major publisher, we have seen where he relied upon some white support. To continue the tone of his early writings Griggs would have certainly killed whatever writing ambitions he had. White readership and patronage would not have come his way.

There still was another side to this lack of access to major publishers for the black author during the period. Since there was a dearth of African American writers who were in print, most of the black scholars had to rely upon the perspectives that whites gave in their publications. Thus, just out of a lack of divergent publications, black scholars were forced to drink deeply from fountains that poured forth white perspectives. Undoubtedly, this helped to make some of Griggs' ideas appear ridiculous in light of later scholarship. For example, unquestioningly, he accepted the premise that the Negro was a new race, still in its infantile status. Griggs believed this because this was what he read. Likewise, his view of African history was negative and inadequate because of this same causative factor.

He was influenced by Charles Darwin, Thomas Huxley, Herbert Spencer, Benjamin Kidd, and others. All of these writers presented their theories from the presumptions that an Anglophile had of the world being shaped from an Euro-centric basis. Among Griggs' scholarly influences the only exception to this rule was W.E.B. DuBois, who he departed from in his older years. Tragically, Griggs like most blacks and whites of his time, was victimized intellectually by not being privy to the wealth of cosmopolitan ideas that posterity later uncovered.[16] Griggs was only able to regurgitate what he had been fed. His intellectual diet had consisted almost exclusively of Euro-centric thought.

Consequently, to simply dismiss Griggs as a money hungry Uncle Tom is to have no consideration for the era in which he lived. One must acknowledge the lack of free expression and education for a southern black man during Griggs' lifetime. Liberation for writing and learning had not come to the African American during that era. He was completely programmed by the dominant culture. Economically and educationally he was a dependent of his adversary. Thus, to label Griggs as a mercenary who betrayed his people is to make a villain out of a victim.

Aside from his times, we must also give proper credit to Griggs for the depth of his philosophical thought. While there were external influences upon him such as monetary problems and racial oppression, it is most evident that he reasoned himself into his final position. Monetary needs alone could not have prompted the logical, methodical thoughts that Griggs espoused. Only careful reflection could have produced his ideas on social efficiency.

ʌs a youthful idealist, Griggs wrote from the viewpoint of a crusader. He told all that was wrong with American society so far as the African American was concerned. He criticized lynching and disfranchisement. He called for fairness and equality for the ebony-skinned American.

However, age and experience taught Griggs that wrongs were not going to be righted simply because he brought them to the public's attention. Therefore, as an older crusader he replaced idealism with pragmatism. Rather than just stating what needed to be done in the area of race relations, he laid out a plan whereby it might be achieved through social efficiency.

While Griggs was a realist in counselling his race not to look to the government for help, he was overly optimistic in his call for interracial cooperation. He gave only a minimal effort to interracial cooperation and dwelt upon what the Negro must do to win the goodwill of whites. Thus, while under the guise of pragmatism, Griggs was unrealistic to think that the African American alone could bring about a solution to America's race problem. He put forth no demands whatsoever upon whites. According to his plan for interracial cooperation the Negro had to do it all. Such a view gives the impression that the black man was the sole cause of racial misunderstanding.

Undoubtedly, Griggs wrote in this manner because his thinking had been conditioned by the dominant authors of the period. Such writers as his early opponent, Thomas Nelson Page, had consistently referred to the race problem as "the Negro problem." Such epithets conveyed the impression that the Negro was the only cause of an American racial problem.

Yet, there was an experiential basis for Griggs' later philosophy. The dominant influence upon him at this period was the example of Booker T. Washington's success in establishing Tuskegee Institute. Griggs saw Washington skillfully use flattery on the white South to win support for his school. Griggs became convinced that such an approach was more productive than the early confrontational efforts of DuBois. In fact, he had even seen DuBois abandon the original militancy of the Niagara Movement for the biracial moderation of the National Association for the Advancement of Colored People. Thus, Griggs forsook the methods of the Harvard educated DuBois for that of the Hampton educated Washington.

Sutton Griggs' efforts to winning support from the Southern Baptist Convention for the American Baptist Theological Seminary gave him a personal experience that proved the Washington approach worked. Consequently, when he came to Memphis and decided to build Tabernacle Baptist Church into an institutional congregation, he pursued and even escalated his accommodationist overtures toward the white community. To win support for his venture, like Washington had done in

Alabama, he tried to show white Memphians that Tabernacle would be able to train workers for their benefit.

While making overtures toward white society, Griggs was able also to persuade many influential blacks that he had a viable answer to the race issue. Thus, not only whites, but blacks as well, supported Griggs verbally and financially in his pioneering efforts.

Thus, to characterize Griggs as a purchased mouthpiece for white interests is to ignore the support that he also gleaned among blacks. While David Tucker goes to great lengths to show Griggs had white support, he neglects to mention the black support that always accompanied his ventures. Thus, in reality Griggs did enact a measure of interracial cooperation. His later ventures always received biracial financing and endorsements.

In addition, Tucker again went to great lengths to demonstrate that Griggs and Tabernacle received financial backing from the Memphis Chamber of Commerce. While this is true, it must also be understood that these were not unconditional gifts. Rather, as was pointed out previously, the Chamber's Industrial Welfare Committee only made matching contributions to organizations that were engaged in self-help. Thus, the monies that Tabernacle received from that source were more like a grant that was predicated upon an institution's proven objectives and capabilities. Based on the Industrial Welfare Committee's report, they did not buy Griggs' pronouncements against black northern migration. Rather, they just simply endorsed a position that the clergyman already held.

Furthermore, his convictions on this matter were not the result of financial expediency. Instead, Griggs arrived at his conclusion as a result of analytical thought. As was discussed in chapter six, Griggs had studied the association between Negro mortality and the northern urban migration. He saw that death was premature for too many African Americans in the northern cities. Thus, it would appear that this reason and not financial gain prompted Griggs to advise southern blacks to remain domiciled in the southland, which he thought was better suited to the African American.

In addition to racial concerns, it is evident from his theological metamorphosis that Griggs' change from his earlier position was the result of maturing thoughts. While not completely abandoning natural selection, Griggs did come to a greater appreciation for man's ability to change. This was illustrative of his closer alliance with fundamentalism in his later years. While one could not accurately describe him as a "Bible thumper", it is clear that the later Griggs relied more upon biblical authority than he did as a younger thinker. There was less citing of scientific theory and more biblical citations in his older years. He even came to the point where he parted company with some of Darwin and Huxley's teachings on genetics as a final determinant in human behavior.

Instead, he came to see the importance that environment had upon character development.

Consequently, the mere fact that Griggs changed not only his racial views but theological perspective as well shows that something more profound than the enticement of finance was the root cause of the metamorphosis. Again, it is necessary to point out that the change was a result of Griggs reasoning himself into his final position. Careful analytical thought, combined with life experiences caused him to rethink his earlier positions not only on social concerns, but theological concepts as well. Thus, Griggs' sojourn was predicated upon his own inner reflection rather than the mere prospect of "filthy lucre."

To ignore this causative factor is to snub the essence of his contribution. Griggs spent his life trying to fathom America's racial dilemma. Trial and error, as well as constant study influenced his conceptional flexibility. Consequently, the more experiences Griggs had the more he expanded his thinking. From his own adventure in winning support for American Baptist Theological Seminary, he became convinced that the African American would fare better through compromise rather than confrontation. History had taught him that the African American must not expect the government nor any other outside agency to come to his aid.

His vision for Tabernacle was a reflection of his self-help concept. Rather than begging the city government for jobs and a recreational facility for blacks in South Memphis, Griggs set out to accomplish these things through his church.

Although some of Griggs' overtures toward whites were hard for African Americans to stomach, no one can accuse him of ever forsaking the love he had for his people. In fact, the closest suggestion of any betrayal by him came from the hearsay evidence introduced by Tucker as he quoted from Fred Hutchins' second hand account.[17]

Needless to say, this is not sufficient data upon which to judge Griggs' loyalty. For just as Hutchins reportedly heard that Griggs defended lynching by repeating a southern white platitude, there is also other hearsay evidence that said Griggs joined forces with T.O. Fuller and others to protest what they considered as unacceptable the first proposed name for Booker T. Washington High School in Memphis.[18]

Yet, while one can counterbalance secondary sources with secondary citations this is not the most accurate form of historical scholarship. Consequently, one must not persist in this type of documentation.

Instead, once again note must be taken of the evidence presented in Chapter Five. There, the reader saw where Griggs even after his efforts at interracial cooperation continued to attempt to convince the white South to pay fair wages to black workers. Furthermore, as late as 1925, his publications continued to condemn lynching.[19]

Thus, the primary sources demonstrate that Griggs never lost the love he had for his people. At a time when the black press throughout the nation carried advertisements for bleaching creams and hair straighteners, Sutton Griggs remained a proud black man. In none of his writings is there a hint that he ever wished to alter the physical appearance of the race. In fact, it is consistent throughout his publications that he never considered amalgamation as a possible solution to the race issue.

Griggs then does not change in what he wishes for black people. Both the young and older Griggs wished to see the African American progress and attain international elevation and acceptance. The only change in Griggs' philosophy was in the method used to attain the desired goal of black uplift.

The change in method was only pursued because his earlier confrontational strategy was not effective in advancing the race. Observation of empirical historical evidence convinced the thinker that the success of black progress would only come through compromise.

The intensity of Griggs' reasoning can be seen in the fact that despite his change in method he still synthesized scientific and liberal theological views with his social philosophy. As a result, his philosophy of social efficiency was as much a product of natural observation of flora and fauna as it was of social experience. Consequently, to only characterize Sutton Griggs in his later years as being a co-opted Negro is at best superficial. Griggs was a thinker who was handicapped by living in an era that limited his potential.

The limitation was placed upon him as a student and a teacher. The majority of the publications he read reflected an Euro-centric perspective that scorned Africa and her history. As a teacher, his influence was squashed through a denial from publishing houses. The enormous expense born by himself for his private printings kept him economically depressed.

On the latter point, Griggs must be held accountable at least in part. If his early writings were the failures he set forth in *The Story of My Struggles,* why would he persist in throwing good money after bad? Even if he continued to write, why would he produce so many copies in the first printing? It would have been more prudent to publish a minimal amount, sell them, and then reprint as the need arose. This certainly would seem to have been the logical plan after it became clear to the author that his books only sold through personal contact.

Perhaps he persisted in the overproduction of his printed copies because he had overrated himself. It would seem that Griggs was better known in Tennessee and black Baptist circles than he was generally throughout the nation. However, his voluminous printings would tend to suggest he never thought of his influence as primarily limited to such quarters. Consequently, it seems reasonable to assume that at least occasionally his ego was greater than his business sense.

Undoubtedly, it was this same lack of business acumen that led to the foreclosure on Tabernacle. Lack of attention to the church's income and an inordinate debt burden did not allow any room for the strain of the Great Depression.

In the final analysis, Sutton E. Griggs was a tragic figure. He had such high hopes for his race and America. Yet, it was not for his era to see these hopes materialize. In many ways his life represented the country during a time of transition. The era was a time of conflict and contrast. Science was emerging to challenge the traditions of Christian fundamentalism. Speculative thought was being adopted as a companion to orthodoxy. The adoptive process was not painless. Many in the South refused to accept any aspects of a marriage between religion and science. When some did, they twisted the two into Social Darwinism, which was used to perpetuate and justify racism and imperialism. Furthermore, in racial matters, the African American was attempting to rise from the losses suffered from the Compromise of 1877 which brought Reconstruction to a close. It was a time when southern communities accepted discrimination, lynching, disfranchisement, and white supremacy as a way of life. Thus, just as Griggs' personal life contained tragedy, so did the time in which he lived.

At least Sutton E. Griggs was a representation of a segment of the society that attempted to address the problems. He ventured to do this even at the risk of criticism, ostracism, and ultimate disappointment. Indeed, it is time that posterity recognize one who attempted to grapple with the social evils of his day.

NOTES

[1] National Baptist Convention. *Journal of the 18th Annual Session* (Kansas City, Missouri, 1898), p. 16.

[2] *The Commercial Appeal,* August 16, 1925, p. 9.

[3] James Weldon Johnson, The Burning of Ell Person at Memphis, Report made for the National Association for the Advancement of Colored People, p. 8.

[4] *The Commercial Appeal,* September 14, 1919, p. 25.

[5] *The Commercial Appeal,* August 16, 1925, p. 1.

[6] *Ibid.*

[7] *Ibid.*

[8] G. P. Hamilton, *The Bright Side of Memphis* (Memphis: by Author, 1908), p. 9.

[9] Interview conducted by Randolph Meade Walker, with Elder Blair T. Hunt, Pastor Emeritus, Mississippi Boulevard Christian Church, Memphis, Tennessee, October 22, 1975. The examples which Hunt offered are not examples of Memphis' uniqueness, for they occurred during Reconstruction, the high point of black political progress throughout the South.

[10] Interview conducted by Randolph Meade Walker, with Rev. A. McEwen Williams, Pastor, St. John Baptist Church, Memphis, Tennessee, October 15, 1975.

[11] *The Commercial Appeal,* March 28, 1919, p. 8.

[12] *Ibid.*

[13]Herbert Aptheker, who edited *The Education of Black People: Ten Critiques, 1906-1960* (New York and London: Monthly Review Press, 1973) was responsible for this posthumous publication of DuBois' work. In the introduction, Aptheker chronicles the struggle that DuBois had as late as the early forties in trying to get this work published. The University of North Carolina Press stamped the manuscript "Ret'd to author 2-19-41. Press unable to publish at present for financial reasons" (ix).

[14]John Hope Franklin and Alfred A. Moss, Jr. *From Slavery to Freedom: A History of Negro Americans* (New York: Alfred A. Knopf, 1988), p. 338.

[15]Zora Neale Hurston in her early years generated much criticism from blacks just as Griggs did in his late works. For more details on this phase of Hurston's career see Marie Milam, "Zora Neale Hurston: A Modern Analysis" (Memphis: Unpublished Study).

[16]Essentially modern scholarship has stated that no one group of people has exclusively contributed to human civilization. Representative of this new view is that of the Annales school of historians who interpret the past from the perspective of the world reacting to climate, geography, and material needs. An example of cosmopolitan creativity is the belief that agriculture was discovered repetitively around the globe without the benefit of cultural diffusion.

[17]David M. Tucker, *Black Pastors and Leaders: Memphis, 1819-1972* (Memphis: Memphis State University Press, 1975), p. 81.

[18]Interview by Randolph Meade Walker, with Grover Mosley, local historian, Memphis, Tennessee, February 9, 1990. According to Mosley the first proposed name was the Negro Normal and Industrial High School. What prompted the ministers' protest was the city's opposition to honoring Booker T. Washington because of his race.

[19]Sutton E. Griggs, *Paths of Progress; or Co-operation Between the Races, A Series of Addresses, Articles, and Essays* (Memphis: National Public Welfare League, 1925), p. 42.

APPENDIX

In the following photographs one can see a sampling of the racial climate in which Sutton E. Griggs had to live and work. It is most evident that throughout the country and especially in the South that segregation and black oppression were taken for granted.

The illustration below and on the next page is of a post card (front and rear) that was mailed in 1922.

Figure I. KKK (front of postcard)
Courtesy Mississippi Valley Collection—Memphis State University

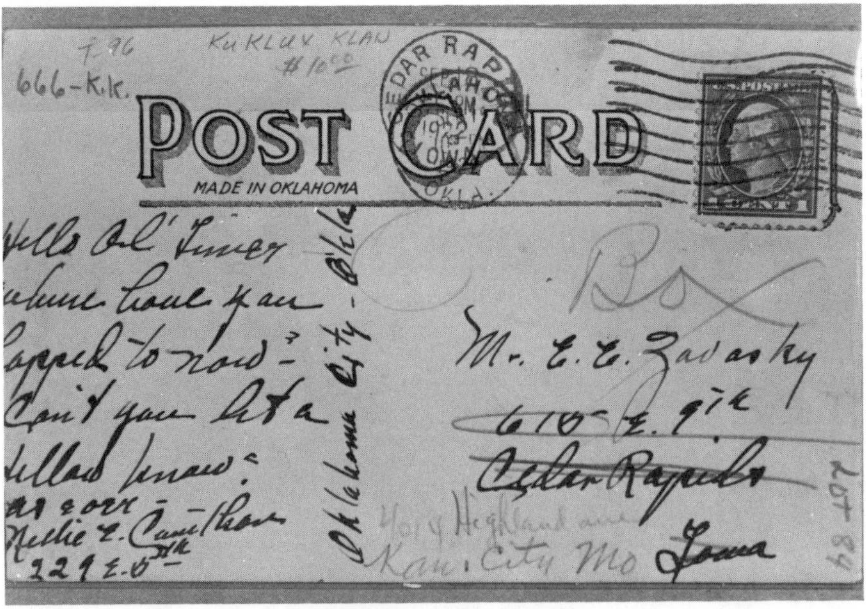

Figure II. Rear of postcard
Courtesy Mississippi Valley Collection - Memphis State University

Figures III and IV demonstrate not only segregation, but the racial connection with the division of labor. White collar jobs were primarily filled by white males as shown in these photographs.

Figure III. White Male Clerk Typists
Knights of Columbus War Activities School (W.W.I) Memphis, Tennessee.
Photo by C. H. Poland—Courtesy Mississippi Valley Collection—
Memphis State University.

Figure IV. White Male Mechanical Drawing
Knights of Columbus War Activities School (W.W.I) Memphis, Tennessee.
Photo by C. H. Poland—Courtesy Mississippi Valley Collection—
Memphis State University.

On the opposite end of the spectrum were the manual trades which were dominated by black workers. The two photographs below and on the following page show an auto mechanics class that is all black and a somewhat more dignified tailoring class that is also all black.

Figure V. All Black Mechanic's Class
Knights of Columbus War Activities School (W.W.I.) Memphis, Tennessee.
Photo by C. H. Poland—courtesy Mississippi Valley Collection—
Memphis State University.

Figure VI. All Black Tailoring Class
Knights of Columbus War Activities School (W.W.I.) Memphis, Tennessee.
Photo by C. H. Poland—courtesy Mississippi Valley Collection—
Memphis State University.

This photograph was taken following the close of World War I. It provides a strange synthesis between the contemporary troops of the United States and a reunion of Confederate veterans. In the rear standing tall atop his horse is a statute of the Confederate General Nathan Bedford Forest.

Figure VII. Confederate Reunion
Courtesy of Mississippi Valley Collection—Memphis State University

One of the few blacks in Memphis whose memory was commemorated by an historic monument was Tom Lee after whom a park was named. Aside from the names of E. H. Crump and his committee, the inscription on the obleski reads:

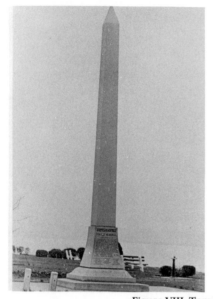

Tom Lee Memorial

A very worthy negro
Tom Lee with his boat
"Zev" saved thirty-two
lives when the steamer
U.S. Normal sank about
twenty miles below
Memphis May 8, 1925—
but he has a finer
monument than this—
an invisible one—a
monument of kindliness,
generosity, courage
and bigness of heart.
His good deeds were
scattered everywhere
that day and into
eternity. This
monument erected by
the grateful people of
Memphis.

Figure VIII. Tom Lee Memorial
Courtesy of Mississippi Valley Collection—Memphis State University

This scene depicts the pivotal period in which Sutton Griggs experienced the coming of age of science. Here we see the blending of the old and the new modes of transportation. The picture clearly shows the acceptance of the automobile. However, the era also still retained a substantial number of horse drawn carriages. In many ways Sutton Griggs was a product of the conflict between the old and the new. Just as these horses and automobiles are in the same picture, Griggs blended science and the Bible into a common system of thought.

Figure IX. Horses and Automobiles
Courtesy Mississippi Valley Collection — Memphis State University

Further changes in the period can be seen in this photograph of the Lycelm Theatre in Memphis. In the heart of the theologically conservative Bible Belt there was a long line waiting to go in to see Pete Pate & Girls and Syncopated Steppers & Beauty Chorus. Ironically in the same age in the bluff city, revivalists like Billy Sunday drew impressive crowds. Thus, just as the period was a conflict between technology and conventional animal power, it also was a time of confrontation between fundamental Christianity and growing urban secular pursuits.

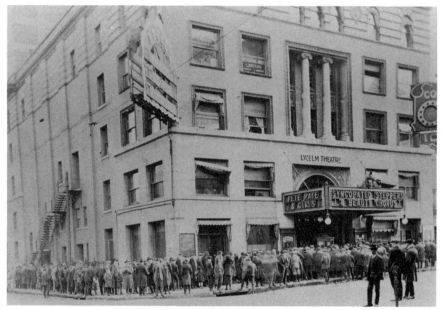

Figure X. Lycelm Theatre
Courtesy Mississippi Valley Collection—Memphis State University

During the early twentieth century Memphis became known as the "Mule Capital of the World." An ever present companion of this lowly beast of burden was the black man. The following scene was quite common during the time of Sutton Griggs' residence.

Figure XI. Negroes on Mules
Courtesy Memphis Room—Memphis/Shelby County Public Library
and Information Center.

Together the Negro and the mule played a big part in the Mid South's cotton culture. This role did not remain confined to rural fields. Here we see a mule cart transporting cotton bales from the fields to the wharf where they were loaded aboard a Mississippi Riverboat.

The typical mule cart which transported the bales from the fields to the Wharf

Figure XII. Negro driving a mule cart
Courtesy Memphis Room—Memphis/Shelby County Public Library
and Information Center.

The black man even exercised a skilled trade in regards to the mule. Here an African American blacksmith is shown putting shoes on a mule.

Figure XIII. Negro putting shoes on a mule
Courtesy Memphis Room—Memphis/Shelby County Public Library
and Information Center

A major contributor to northern migration was southern floods that destroyed crops and any hopes of black economic stability. One of these floods that desecrated the Mid-South occurred in 1912. In the following photograph we see mule drawn wagons playing a helpful role in rescuing African Americans and their belongings during this natural calamity.

Figure XIV. Rescue of 1912 Flood Victims
Courtesy Memphis Room—Memphis/Shelby County Public Library
and Information Center

The desperation of the 1912 flood victims can be seen in the grim faces of these refugees. They were temporarily housed at Camp Crump during May 1912.

Figure XV. Flood victims
Courtesy Memphis Room—Memphis/Shelby County Public Library
and Information Center

The desperation among black people during the 1912 flood was not confined to males. Here we see both women and men lined up awaiting aid during this hardship.

Figure XVI. Female and Male Flood Victims
Courtesy Memphis Room—Memphis/Shelby County Public Library
and Information Center

Highlights From the Life of Sutton E. Griggs

1872 .... Born in Chatfield, Texas on June 19th
1885 .... Converted and baptized into the Baptist Church
1890 .... Graduated from Bishop College in Marshall, TX
1893 .... Graduated from Richmond Theological Seminary
(now Virginia Union University)
1897 .... Married Emma J. Williams on May 10th
1899 .... Published *Imperium in Imperio*
1900 .... Called as pastor of First Baptist Church, Berkley,
Virginia
1901 .... Published *Overshadowed*
1902 .... Called as pastor of First Baptist Church, East
Nashville, Tennessee
1902 .... Published *Unfettered*
1905 .... Published *The Hindered Hand*
1907 .... Published *The One Great Question*
1908 .... Published *Pointing the Way*
1909 .... Published *The Race Question in a New Light*
1910 .... Published *Wisdom's Call*
1911 .... Published *Beyond the End*
1913 .... Called as pastor of Tabernacle Baptist Church,
Memphis, Tennessee
1914 .... Published *The Story of My Struggles*
1916 .... Published *According to Law, or Life's Demands*
1921 .... Published *Light on Racial Issues*
1922 .... Published *Meeting the Great Test*
1923 .... Published *Guide to Racial Greatness*
1924 .... Published *Kingdom Builder's Manual*
1925 .... Elected as President of American Baptist
Theological Seminary on April 8th
1925 .... Published *Paths of Progress*
1926 .... Published *Triumph of the Simple Virtues; or the
Life Story of John L. Webb*
1926 .... Resigned as President of American Baptist
Theological Seminary on October 1st
1929 .... Published *Proper Approach to the Race Question
in the South*
1930 .... Called as pastor of Hopewell Baptist Church,
Denison, Texas
1933 .... Died in Houston, Texas on January 3rd

BIBLIOGRAPHY

Alkalimat, Abdul and Associates. *Introduction to Afro-American Studies: A Peoples College Primer.* Chicago: Twenty-first Century Books and Publications, 1986.

Banks, Elizabeth L. "The American Negro and His Place." *Nineteenth Century,* September, 1899, pp. 459-74.

The Bible.

Bone, Robert A. *The Negro Novel in America.* Revised ed. New Haven and London: Yale University Press, Inc., 1965.

Brewster, William Herbert. *Tribute: The Life of Dr. William Herbert Brewster.* Memphis: The Brewster House of Sermon, Songs, Christian Literature and Dramatic Arts, 1982.

Brown, Claude. *Manchild in the Promised Land.* New York: The MacMillan Co., 1965.

Brown, Sterling. *The Negro in American Fiction.* Washington: The Associates in Negro Folk Education, 1937.

Bruce, Philip A. *The Plantation Negro as a Freeman.* New York: G. P. Putnam's Sons, 1889.

Chamber of Commerce Journal, II (December, 1919).

Chicago Defender. January 7, 1933.

The Commercial Appeal. January 13, 1898.

The Commercial Appeal. April 13, 1913.

The Commercial Appeal. April 17, 1916.

The Commercial Appeal. July 1, 1916.

The Commercial Appeal. July 9, 1916.

The Commercial Appeal. March 28, 1919.

The Commercial Appeal. September 14, 1919.

The Commercial Appeal. December 21, 1919.

The Commercial Appeal. March 30, 1924.

The Commercial Appeal. August 16, 1925.

The Commercial Appeal. December 15, 1925.

The Commercial Appeal. October 19, 1926.

The Commercial Appeal. August 20, 1975.

Daniels, Jonathan. "He Suits Memphis." *Saturday Evening Post,* June 10, 1939, pp. 22-23, 48.

Dixon, Thomas, Jr. *The Clansman: An Historical Romance of the Ku Klux Klan.* New York: Grosset & Dunlap, 1905.

Dixon, Thomas, Jr. *The Leopard's Spots: A Romance of the White Man's Burden 1865-1900.* New York: Doubleday, Page & Co., 1902.

DuBois, W. E. B. *The Education of Black People: Ten Critiques, 1906-1960.* Edited by Herbert Aptheker. New York and London: Monthly Review Press, 1973.

DuBois, W. E. B. *The Souls of Black Folk.* Greenwich, Conn.: Fawcett Publications, Inc., 1961.

Eggleston, Edward. *The Ultimate Solution of the American Negro Problem.* Boston: The Gorham Press, 1913.

131

Esler, Anthony. *The Human Venture: The Great Enterprise, A World History to 1500.* Englewood Cliffs, N.J.: Prentice-Hall, Inc., 1986.

Fitts, Leroy. *A History of Black Baptists.* Nashville: Broadman Press, 1985.

Fleming, Robert E. "Sutton E. Griggs: Militant Black Novelist." *Phylon, XXXIV* (March, 1973), pp. 73-77.

Franklin, John Hope and Moss, Alfred A., Jr. *From Slavery to Freedom: History of Negro Americans.* 6th ed. New York: Alfred A. Knopf, 1980.

Frazier, E. Franklin. *The Negro Church in America.* New York: Schocken Books, 1964.

Fuller, T. O. *History of the Negro Baptists of Tennessee.* Memphis: By author, 1936.

Fullinwider, S. P. *The Mind and Mood of Black America.* Homewood, Illinois: The Dorsey Press, 1969.

Gloster, Hugh. "Sutton E. Griggs: Novelist of the New Negro." *Phylon, IV* (fourth quarter, 1943), pp. 335-345.

Griggs, Sutton E. *According to Law, or Life's Demands.* Memphis: National Public Welfare League, 1916.

Griggs, Sutton E. *Beyond the End: Sequel to Wisdom's Call.* Nashville: Orion Publishing Co., 1911.

Griggs, Sutton E. *Cooperative Natures and Social Education, A Philosophy of Civic Life.* Memphis: National Public Welfare League, 1929.

Griggs, Sutton E. *Guide to Racial Greatness; or the Science of Collective Efficiency.* Memphis: National Public Welfare League, 1923.

Griggs, Sutton E. *The Hindered Hand; or the Reign of the Repressionist.* 3rd ed. New York: AMS Press, 1969.

Griggs, Sutton E. *Imperium in Imperio.* Miami: Mnemosyne, 1969.

Griggs, Sutton E. *Kingdom Builder's Manual, Companion Book to Guide to Racial Greatness.* Memphis: National Public Welfare League, 1924.

Griggs, Sutton E. *Light on Racial Issues.* Memphis: The National Public Welfare League, 1921.

Griggs, Sutton E. *Meeting the Great Test: Constructive Criticism of the Negro Race.* Memphis: National Public Welfare League, 1922.

Griggs, Sutton E. "Negroes Steadily Recording Progress." *The Commercial Appeal.* February 28, 1924.

Griggs, Sutton E. *The Negro's Next Step.* Memphis: National Public Welfare League, 1923.

Griggs, Sutton E. *The One Great Question, A Study of Southern Conditions at Close Range.* Philadelphia: Orion Publishing Co., 1907.

Griggs, Sutton E. *Paths of Progress; or Co-operation Between the Races, A Series of Addresses, Articles, and Essays.* Memphis: National Public Welfare League, 1925.

Griggs, Sutton E. *Proper Approach to the Race Question in the South.* Memphis: National Public Welfare League, 1929.

Griggs, Sutton E. *The Race Question in a New Light.* Nashville: Orion Publishing Co., 1909.

Griggs, Sutton E. *The Story of My Struggles.* Memphis: The National Public Welfare League, 1914.

Griggs, Sutton E. *Triumph of the Simple Virtues; or the Life Story of John L. Webb.* Hot Springs, AR.: Messenger, 1926.

Griggs, Sutton E. *Unfettered and Dorlan's Plan.* New York: AMS Press, 1971.

Griggs, Sutton E. *Wisdom's Call.* Nashville: Orion Publishing Co., 1911.

Hamilton, G. P. *The Bright Side of Memphis.* Memphis; by author, 1908.

Hoffman, Frederick L. *Race Traits and Tendencies of the American Negro.* New York: The MacMillan Company, 1896.

Hofstadter, Richard. *Social Darwinism in American Thought.* Revised ed. Boston: Beacon Press, 1955.

Hunt, Blair T. Pastor Emeritus, Mississippi Boulevard Christian Church, Memphis, Tennessee. Interview by Randolph Meade Walker, October 22, 1975.

Johnson, James Weldon. The Burning of Ell Person at Memphis, Report made for the National Association for the Advancement of Colored People.

Jones, Amos. Speech before Memphis Baptist Ministers Association, Memphis, Tennessee, May 30, 1989.

Jordan, Winthrop D. *White Over Black: American Attitudes Toward the Negro, 1550-1812.* Baltimore: Penguin Books, Inc., 1969.

Journal of the Thirty-fifth Annual Session of the National Baptist Convention. Chicago, 1915.

July, Robert W. *A History of the African People.* New York: Charles Scribner's Sons, 1970.

Lincoln, Abraham. *Speeches and Writings, 1859-1865.* New York: Literary Classics of the United States, 1989.

Logan, Rayford. *The Betrayal of the Negro: From Rutherford B. Hayes to Woodrow Wilson.* London: Collier-MacMillan Ltd., 1965.

Logan, Rayford W. and Winston, Michael R., eds. *Dictionary of American Negro Biography.* New York: W. W. Norton & Company, 1982.

Marsden, George M. *Fundamentalism and American Culture: The Shaping of Twentieth-Century Evangelicalism: 1870-1925.* New York: Oxford University Press, Inc., 1989.

Mays, Benjamin E. *The Negro's God; As Reflected in His Literature.* Autheneum ed. New York: Autheneum, 1973.

Meir, August. *Negro Thought in America, 1880-1915.* Ann Arbor: The University of Michigan Press, 1963.

The Memphis Branch National Association for the Advancement of Colored People. Application for Charter, 1917.

Memphis Chamber of Commerce Journal, IV (May, 1921).

Memphis World. September 25, 1931.

Milam, Marie. "Zora Neale Hurston: A Modern Analysis." Unpublished study, Memphis, 1990.

Mosley, Grover. Local historian, Memphis, Tennessee. Interview by Randolph Meade Walker, February 9, 1990.

National Baptist Convention. *Journal of Thirty-Eighth Annual Session.* St. Louis, 1918.

National Baptist Convention. *Journal of the Eighteenth Annual Session.* Kansas City, Mo., 1898.

Page, Thomas Nelson. *The Negro: The Southerner's Problem.* New York: Scribner, 1904.

Phillips, Ulrich B. *American Negro Slavery: A Survey of the Supply, Employment and Control of Negro Labor as Determined by the Plantation Regime.* 2nd paperback ed. Baton Rouge: Louisiana State University Press, 1969.

Phillips, Ulrich B. "The Plantation as a Civilizing Factor." *Sewanee Review,* XII (July, 1904), pp. 257-67.

Pittsburgh Courier. November 1, 1930.

Pittsburgh Courier. January 21, 1933.

Powell, Ruth Marie. *Lights and Shadows: The Story of the American Baptist Theological Seminary 1924-64.* Nashville: By the author, 1964.

Roark, Eldon F. Jr. *Memphis Press Scimitar.* January 4, 1933.

"The Search for Adam and Eve." *Newsweek,* January 11, 1988, pp. 46-52.

Tucker, David M. *Black Pastors and Leaders: Memphis, 1819-1972.* Memphis: Memphis State University Press, 1975.

Williams, A. McEwen. Pastor, St. John Baptist Church, Memphis, Tennessee. Interview by Randolph Meade Walker, October 15, 1975.

Woodson, Carter Godwin. *The Mis-Education of the Negro.* Revised ed. Washington: The Associated Publishers, Inc., 1977.

Woodward, C. Vann. *The Strange Career of Jim Crow.* New York: Oxford University Press, 1957.

Ordering Information

Copies of this book and Randolph Meade Walker's first book, *Organization for the Organism: A Survey of Church Positions and Auxiliaries* may be purchased at your local bookstore or New Philadelphia Baptist Church, 533 South Mendenhall Road, Memphis, Tennessee 38117. The phone number is (901) 685-8877.